Knowledge Management in Organisations and in People's Lives

Knowledge Management in Organisations and in People's Lives

Dr Viswanathan Gopalan

GenNext Publication

ISBN : 978-93-8022-296-7

Price : ₹ 540

First Published, 2016

Published by

GenNext Publications
5, Ansari Road
Daryaganj, New Delhi-110002
Phone: 9811692060
E-mail: gennext@hotmail.com

Printed at: G. Print Process, Delhi.

Cataloging in Publication Data—DK

Courtesy: D.K. Agencies (P) Ltd. <docinfo@dkagencies.com>

Gopalan, Viswanathan, author.

Knowledge management in organisation and in people lives/ Dr Viswanathan Gopalan.

pages cm

Includes bibliographical references.

ISBN

1. Knowledge management. 2. Organizational learning. 3. Self-managed learning. I. Title.

HD30.2.G67 2016 DDC 658.4038 23

Contents

Foreword

One of the greatest challenges the human being faces today, in this competitive world, is his compulsion to deal with vast amounts of data and information on a daily basis, in order to survive and stay in the race. What bugs him, however, is the task of finding out what constitutes real knowledge and how he can manage it so that the purpose of leading life and succeeding it remains a possibility.

Dr Viswanathan Gopalan, in this unique book, 'Knowledge Management-In, Organisations and In People's Lives' has discussed with penetrating insights a step-by-step pathway as to how such a knowledge enables one to live with fairness, integrity and human dignity – principles that give us the security to adapt to change and the wisdom as well the power to take advantage of the opportunity that change creates.

This book makes the reader fully aware that knowledge and its management is the crux of managing all issues in life, be at work place or in personal life.

Dr Viswanathan Gopalan has been an engineer, a corporate manager, a professor in management, a trainer and a researcher. He has also been a key member of Vidya Vrikshah, an NGO for helping the Visually Challenged Children. He has authored already one book titled, 'Motivation'-The Essence of Living.

This book on Knowledge Management can be read and appreciated by the academic and research communities, organisations in the public and private domain, and the common man also. The knowledge that Dr Viswanathan has shared in this book with the reader is useful, innovative and inspiring.

-Sd-
Date: 28.10.2015

Dr M. P. Haran
M.A, D.Phil (Economics)
Fellow of the Royal Economic Society of London
Former Resident Director. Marine Authority
Ministry of Commerce & Industry Govt. of India.

Acknowledgements

I acknowledge and thank all my friends, students and colleagues in the Educational Institutions in Pune where I have taught over the last several years of my career, the fellow researchers whom I meet in conferences, who sincerely wished that I should publish the second book of my choice, having published my first in 2014. Their constant reminders have been inspiring and definitely motivating.

Special thanks and appreciation to my loved ones and family members including my dear wife Indira, daughter Sharmila, her husband Arjun and my son Vivek who constantly lent me support and words of appreciation to keep me inspired to finish my job well.

It will not be appropriate if I do not acknowledge the initiative shown and the support given by Shri B P Garg, Director, Gyan Books Pvt Ltd, New Delhi, in ensuring publication of this book by his company. I wish to thank all members of his team from production, publication and marketing who lent active support for the objective.

I wish to congratulate and thank all the readers who read, enjoy and stand to benefit from this book which is intended to enhance their knowledge and wisdom to manage the organisations in which they work and in their personal lives too.

I thank God for giving me this opportunity to serve Humanity by sharing the knowledge I have managed to acquire on this subject,with His Blessings and Grace.

—Dr Viswanathan Gopalan

23 -10-2015
Pune, India

Chapter 1

Introduction to Knowledge Management

"The only true wisdom is in knowing you know nothing."

—***Socrates***

We live to-day in an 'Information Era' where everything that we encounter, everything we are surrounded by, relates to some form of information which someone wishes to read, share or understand for one's own purpose or for the collective benefit of a group of people, small or large. Technology on the internet and tools for documentation and transmission of information has been perfected to an almost near complete stage that proliferation, distribution and sharing of information has become easy even for a school going child or a student.

The globe has shrunk virtually in terms of our ability to communicate with each other using media tools like the TV or radio, devices like the phone, mobile or the computer. The purposes for which the people across the world try and relate to each other can be economic such as trade, social such as events and news, or educational such as distant education from a foreign University or simply health such as availability of a drug for a dreaded disease which is known to cause death and damage to human beings. 'Globalisation' is a term which is used not only for trade and economic relationships across nations, but also perceived and understood in the larger context of man beginning to see the world as a single place to exist, survive and prosper regardless of national boundaries and hence many elected governments accept this notion, except in countries where some form of autocratic rule prevails.

The challenge mankind faces in this improved communication-interaction scenario, however, is, how much of all these transactions constitute useful information, how much is a waste and how much is absolutely useless. Can we distinguish between 'relevant' and 'irrelevant' information or mere 'data' which adds no 'value' to the issues we face in our daily lives?

The biggest challenge, in other words, is to identify useful 'knowledge' from unwanted pieces of data and information. The purpose is to assimilate 'knowledge' in various walks of life which will enhance our productivity, improve our efficiency, make us more innovative and lead better lives. Technology comes in handy for this purpose.

Knowledge management is all about the task of re-inventing knowledge which can be used and re-used for the purpose of accomplishing the ideal of better, efficient and innovative living by identifying 'patterns' from available piles of data and information which can be used for beneficial purposes of existence of the human beings and other forms of lives including the birds, animals and plants we encounter on planet earth. Knowledge management helps us gain wisdom which should eventually lead us to enlightenment and freedom in a spiritual sense. Knowledge management should help us understand even the mysteries of the solar system, the galaxies and the cosmos of which we are a tiny part.

In this chapter of the book, we will start the process of making the reader more aware by introducing him to the very basics of the subject by explaining some of the terms, concepts and purposes of knowledge management. Let us begin our fascinating journey right away without any further delay.

Fundamentals – Data- Information – Knowledge – Wisdom (Ref. 2)

It is worth understanding the meanings of some of the most common words we use in our daily lives, even though we presume that we know already, before we make forays in to bigger concepts in knowledge management.

Data: We constantly hear words like 'Data', 'Data Analysis', 'Data Card', 'Databases' and so on in our modern daily lives, even a non-computer person does. However, we have never stopped to think and reflect upon the real significance and meaning of this term. Data represents a piece of information which by itself has no relevance unless it connects into a relationship with another piece of information such as it. Data is an event in space and time without any context. Some examples of data without any relevance are given below:

1. Vehicle No. MH12 xxxxxxx
2. AAA College of Science
3. YYY Pvt Ltd

Eventhough the above pieces of data may be true and may exist, by themselves, they do not convey any significant meaning and hence have no relevance as information to us. To call anyone of the above data as 'Information' we need to connect or relate the data to another data and establish a meaning in that relationship. The following discussion makes the point clear to us.

Information: Let us take the examples of context free data in order to reframe them as relevant pieces of information.

1. Vehicle No. MH12 xxxxxx belongs to Mr XYZ who lives in Pune.

2. AAA College of Science in Chennai offers PG programmes in Science.
3. YYY Pvt Ltd in Delhi manufactures Two Wheeler Passenger Vehicles.

So, information is available to us when we begin to understand relationship across data. We can expand the examples given above to form more elaborate pieces of information which can be useful to us such as:

1. Vehicle no. MH12 xxxxxx belongs to Mr XYZ who is a Doctor who lives in Pune.
2. AAA College of Science in Chennai offers PG programmes in Science in Chemistry and Physics only.
3. YYY Pvt Ltd in Delhi manufactures Two Wheeler Passenger Vehicles in the Scooter segment.

Data is incomplete in itself while information is total and complete without any further clauses to qualify the same. Now, we come to the most significant part of our ongoing discussion, namely, 'What then is Knowledge'? In what way is it different from 'Information' as we know it now. The following paragraphs will make the reader understand the concept clearly.

Knowledge: Many times we are lead to believe that all information is knowledge. Large bulk of data and information hoodwink us to think that we are acquiring knowledge when we try and assimilate such volumes of information which can sometimes turn out to be junk and worthless. They may end up causing noise and confusion in the person dealing with them than providing clarity and understanding on any topic of importance.

Information of any kind, small or big in size, can be categorised as knowledge only when the person dealing with it can understand 'patterns' underlying any thought which requires an answer from the information presented.

Let us take for example, the database given below in Fig. 1.1, to understand what we have been talking about in the foregoing section. The small database represents information regarding a small company engaging nine persons from various places to generate a software product let us say.

S. No.	*Name*	*Gender*	*Age*	*Qual*	*Place*
1.	Ram	M	30	Ph D	TN
2.	Laxman	M	25	BE	TN
3.	John	M	25	MBA	Goa
4.	Mary	F	25	MBA	Goa
5.	Kevin	M	30	MS	USA
6.	GV	M	60	Ph D	TN
7.	Srinivas	M	30	M Tech	TN
8.	Mrinal	F	25	BE	Maha
9.	Roy	M	30	BE	WB

Fig. 1 (Ref.1)

We are going to explain through this example the differences in the meanings of the terms data, information and knowledge for the reader who is very new to the concept of databases. We can name the database a 'table' in common man's terminology. One look at the table suggests that it contains information regarding the employees of this company. The information pertains to the name, gender, age, qualification and the place of birth of each of these nine employees laid out in the form of columns and rows for the viewer to read.

Each piece of information such as a name, say 'Srinivas', his age '30' and his place of birth 'Tamil Nadu (TN)' represents 'data' because unrelated to each other, each piece has no meaning. When we start relating these tiny bits of data like 'Srinivas aged 30 is from Tamil Nadu', we have generated a useful piece of information from the table which the reader can use for any purpose of his choice. We can store the information in large databases which can consist of several 'related tables' pertaining to different categories of information and that is how a computer stores information in its databases.

Now that we can distinguish between data and information let us dig a little deeper and begin to ask questions regarding knowledge and what it represents. In the example given above, if we ask ourselves, 'What sort of knowledge do we get from looking at the contents of the database?', initially we may come out with answers like, 'We have knowledge regarding the details of the employees of this organisation' which is quite OK but not complete. The knowledge gained this way is not specific and could be vague.

The best way to start acquiring knowledge from the information provided in the database we are looking at will be to look for 'patterns' of information which look alike from the point of view of the search we are making regarding a question in our minds. Let us say, we ask ourselves a question like. 'How many people in this company are aged 35 and above?', we can come out with an answer 'one'. If we just change our question a little bit like. 'How may are below 35', we will find that the answer is 'Eight'. The question is whether both the answers we obtained through these questions constitute knowledge. It has to be understood that we identified patterns of information regarding age like eight people are below the age of 35 and one is above. When we begin to make statements like. 'Most of the guys are young and below 35 while one is old and 60', the pattern of information begins to emerge as 'knowledge'. We can further refine the knowledge we have acquired by asking more questions like, 'How many are from Tamil Nadu? How many are from Goa?' and so on.

The important point, however, remains that all patterns of information we identify may just be classified as information only, unless we re-interpret the patterns of information identified to answer the real queries that we are addressing to satisfy our innermost urges. To illustrate the point we could again turn to the example under consideration. If we ask a question like, 'Why are most of the people from South India and why no one is from North like UP or MP?', more answers will begin to emerge. This would mean that we are shifting from information in to the knowledge domain. The deeper are the questions regarding patterns of information, the deeper is the transition from information to knowledge. So, at one end of the spectrum stands data and at the other end knowledge.

Wisdom: What is the difference between Knowledge and Wisdom? While we can say that knowledge would mean 'understanding' patterns involved in information gathered, wisdom implies extending the idea beyond the knowledge realm and understanding the principles involved. To illustrate this point through an example, let us say that we know that when any object is thrown up, it comes down invariably. Thanks to a great scientist called Newton, we know now that the 'principle' of gravitational force of the earth is very much in operation. Newton was not only a great Scientist, but a very wise man also. No wonder, he is regarded as one of the greatest scientists the world has ever known so far.

In other words, knowledge represents one continuam in which data which has no meaning without a relationship with another piece of data stands at one end, knowledge and wisdom stand at the other end. The continuam extends in to areas of wisdom yet unexplored and not understood completely. Figure 1.2 illustrates this idea of the connection among all the terms we used so far in understanding information and knowledge.

- **Knowledge is a continuam**
- Data
- Information
- Knowledge
- Wisdom

Fig. 1.2

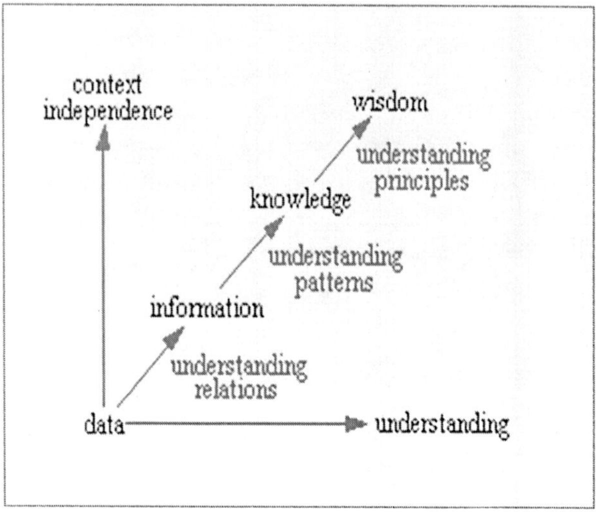

Fig. 1.3 (Ref.1)

Essentially, when we traverse from data to knowledge, wisdom and beyond, our understanding of how events happen around us, why they happen and what binds them in common. When we expand the quest for acquisition of knowledge and wisdom in to the realms of the energy sources around us and the cosmos, we make forays in to the area of knowledge of the self and spirituality. We have spared a chapter later on for discussing some of the concepts in spirituality in the context of knowledge acquisition and management for useful living. Figure 3 illustrates the connection between knowledge and understanding. It is merely symbolic and not absolute.

We see from the above diagram that data represents minimum level of understanding for the human being. Data also is context sensitive. As our understanding improves from data to information, we begin to see the correlation or relationships across pieces of data and this leads to greater understanding of the information we handle. Incidentally, the information we deal with becomes more applicable to many similar contexts and hence the understanding becomes less context sensitive, if not fully.

As we discussed in earlier paragraphs, when we drift from information to knowledge, we become aware of patterns of information we are dealing with. Our attention shifts from specific bits of information to the commonalities involved and the reasons for the same, constituting knowledge. Understanding of the information becomes less context sensitive and more universal. All these transformations are subtle and pleasant. The knowledge seeker begins to be rewarded for his searches and probes while he emerges more and more knowledgeable. He becomes a knowledge worker, a knowledge champion and finally a knowledge Guru in the making.

When a knowledgeable person becomes more aware of the reasons as to why certain patterns of information arise again and again in a collection of data pieces in a database, and would not be satisfied till the reasons are absolutely analysed and understood, he becomes wiser in learning. His understanding of events or data or information around him loses context almost completely. He shifts from knowledge to wisdom and possibly from wisdom into areas of comprehension which could unravel to him principles of universal laws, scientific discoveries and philosophical truths in the ultimate spectrum of knowledge. He becomes a 'Seeker' then. Whether he likes it or not, whether he believes in spirituality and enlightenment or not, he, in that state or 'context', is knocking at the door of the 'unknown' and the 'purpose of life'. The Author has devoted a full chapter on 'Spirituality-Enlightenment' at the end of the book to explain the importance of the quest for knowledge and its connection to the search of the 'Human being' for 'Fulfilment, Content and the Purpose of Life'. The reader is encouraged to read the last chapter carefully, enjoy and derive benefit and satisfaction.

Summary

We have seen in the foregoing sections of this chapter that data represents unrelated pieces of information, while information emerges when relationships among pieces of data are understood.

Knowledge is gained when patterns in information are appreciated and understood while wisdom is acquired when the knowledge seeker delves deeper in to the why's of the knowledge patterns he confronts in order to gain wisdom. In other words, information relates to description, definition or perspective (what, who, when, where), knowledge comprises strategy, practice method or approach (how) and wisdom embodies principle, insight and moral (why). He is then ready to continue his journey in search of 'Truth' and 'The Purpose of Life'. We hope the reader has understood these basics of the concept of knowledge. He is now ready to understand the intricacies of knowledge management starting from the next chapter.

References

1. Malhotra, Yogis. (1998). Knowledge Management, Knowledge Organisations and Knowledge Workers: A View from the Front Lines [WWW document]. URL: http://www. brint. com/interview/maeil. htm
2. Dr Viswanathan Gopalan, 'Knowledge Management, Challenges in the IT Era', ISSN Journal, 2014, ASM Group, Pune.

Chapter 2

Definition and Meaning of Terms in Knowledge Management

"Any fool can know. The point is to understand."

—Albert Einstein

Definition of Knowledge Management (Ref. 1)

Definition 1

"Knowledge Management refers to strategies and structures for maximising return on intellectual and information resources. Because intellectual capital exists in both tacit form (human education, experience and expertise) and explicit form (documents, data). Knowledge Management depends on both cultural and technological processes of creation, collection, sharing, recombination and reuse of knowledge. The goal is to create a new value by improving the efficiency and effectiveness of individual and collaborative knowledge work while increasing innovation and sharpening decision making."

Definition 2

"Knowledge Management is the practise of harnessing and exploiting intellectual capital to gain competitive advantage and customer commitment through efficiency, innovation, faster and more effective decision making."

From the foregoing definitions, certain facts come to our immediate attention. They are:

1. Knowledge management involves human intellectual capital. Intellectual capabilities of the human beings involved in the Knowledge Management Processes are utilised for maximising return in terms of information and knowledge assimilation.
2. The experience and knowledge of the people available in tacit form in the minds of people are captured in the form of explicit documents, data and stored in devices such as even a computer and its memory a manner that will enable us to re-use the knowledge so as to improve productivity, effectiveness and efficiency of the entire environment while contributing to improved innovation and decision making.
3. One of the main objectives of practising Knowledge Management by any organisation or business is to improve its competitiveness and customer commitment through the advantages mentioned such as efficiency, effectiveness, innovativeness and rapid decision making.

The following important processes are bound to be seen in any organisation or institution claiming to practise effective Knowledge Management. (Ref 3, 4, 5, 6)

1. Knowledge creation
2. Knowledge capture
3. Knowledge storage
4. Knowledge re-creation from stored knowledge
5. Knowledge sharing
6. Knowledge re-use for improving efficiency, innovation and decision making

The sustained practise of the above processes will automatically enable the organisations to be more customer oriented and competitive. In the following paragraphs we will discuss some of the principles involved in knowledge generation or knowledge creation.

Types of Knowledge – Tacit and Explicit

As mentioned in the definition of knowledge management, we are always dealing in our lives, two distinct kind of knowledge, regardless of the sources from which they are made available. They are (1) Tacit knowledge available in the minds of individuals and (2) Explicit knowledge available in books, scriptures, nowadays in computers in their storage mediums, memory devices, on internet websites downloaded on to accessible files on the computer and printed later on for our convenient reading at leisure and so on.

Tacit knowledge which is available in the minds of individuals is difficult to tap. It is difficult because the individual with knowledge in a specific area of expertise or excellence must motivate himself to share his knowledge with others or the environment and the people around must motivate him by recognising and rewarding him to share. Either way the knowledge gets passed on to others for their benefit. The others in turn, when they pass on this hard earned knowledge to many others and a cycle on creation is created, the society, in turn, gains. If the tacit knowledge thus obtained is converted into an explicit format which can be proliferated into many, then we are facilitating this knowledge creation and re-creation cycle for the re-use and re-deployment for advantageous purposes of the society. Thus, there are four options of knowledge conversion available to mankind for the purpose of sharing and re-use They are mentioned below.

1. Tacit to Tacit Knowledge Conversion
2. Tacit to Explicit Knowledge Conversion
3. Explicit to Tacit Knowledge Conversion
4. Explicit to Explicit Knowledge Conversion

Tacit to Tacit Knowledge Conversion: Socialisation

One of the most powerful human learning capacities is through socialisation, observing behaviour by others and copying their behaviours and beliefs. Humans learn to speak and survive in their culture almost entirely by socialisation. Psychologists talk about how reward and punishment are at the root of learning, but in fact, we often learn by observing how others are rewarded and punished for their behaviour. For example, if you are new to a group, and some one in the group does a behaviour that triggers a negative non-verbal reaction in the other members of the group, you learn immediately, and often unconsciously, not to follow that behaviour.

Example of this type of behaviour in knowledge management is the way a disciple learns from the master all that the master has learned in his life. Just by being near the master, observing him, learning from him sometimes by listening to his advice and teachings, the disciple inherits the knowledge of the master, which he can later on in his life, transfer to his disciples in either a tacit or even an explicit form in writing. Another example of knowledge transfer through socialisation can be a mother transferring her knowledge in looking after household affairs like cooking, washing, cleaning, gardening etc., to a daughter growing up in the home, under her guidance, from childhood. A tennis coach helping his disciple learn skills in playing through tacit knowledge transfer is yet another example. These examples are enough to illustrate and explain the concept of socialisation as a means of knowledge transfer in knowledge management techniques.

Tacit to Explicit Knowledge Conversion: Articulation

A researcher transferring all the knowledge he has gained while doing research on to a manual or a book for the benefit of fellow researchers or for public to read, understand and gain in knowledge, is an example of the process of articulation in play in the area of knowledge management. The advantage of this type of knowledge transfer is that the knowledge of one person can reach out to a vast majority of people easily. Nowadays, with the availability of tools like the computer and the internet, the process has become a lot faster and easier. E-mails and applications available on even a device like a mobile enable fast transfer of tacit knowledge in an explicit form from one place on earth to another place in a matter of seconds.

Wikipedia is an example of an encyclopaedia containing vast magnitudes of knowledge stored in an explicit form accessible on the net at the click of a button. All this has been possible owing to advances in technology in recent times.

Explicit to Tacit Knowledge Conversion: Internalisation

Let us imagine that a teacher in a college uses presentation materials on a board and nowadays, a power point slide made from a computer application, to explain portions of a chapter under discussion. The teacher, using the tool expands on his thoughts on the topic. The students, on the other hand, are busy, listening to him, and absorbing the inputs given by him in to their memory cells in the brain so that they can understand and recall the matter, later on, for re-use in an appropriate situation in an appropriate manner such as, say, writing an assignment or writing an examination.

What has taken place in the first instance is a process called internalisation which is part of learning. The explicit knowledge available on the slides was presented by the teacher in an explicit form through words and explanations to the students who absorbed the knowledge of the teacher in a tacit manner or form in to their minds for re-use or re-production at a later date in to an explicit form on an assignment booklet or an examination paper.

Scriptures were used in the earlier days to store tacit knowledge of learned people in explicit form. Books are used even to-day to transmit tacit knowledge of experts in an explicit format to the readers improve their knowledge in a tacit manner for re-use by them later on for beneficial purposes. Technology has advanced. Computer servers store even books in web sites for reading, downloads and sharing in explicit manner among viewers in order to contribute to the tacit understanding of subjects of various nature and knowledge assimilation and improvement.

Explicit to Explicit Knowledge Conversion: Combination

When the information or knowledge stored in a folder or a file or a website on a computer is downloaded on to a compact disc or printed through a printer on to a paper, we are essentially converting explicit knowledge into explicit forms. This process is called combination. Combination can involve operation such as combining explicit forms of knowledge such as articles, research papers or book chapters into a final edited book format. Owing to the availability of computer-based technology devices and applications, combination has become an easy and common process among knowledge people for sharing, distribution and re-use of knowledge, which is the prime objective of the knowledge management exercise.

Knowledge Assets (Ref. 2)

We have, so far, dealt with and understood the definition of knowledge management, the meaning of it, types of knowledge such as tacit and explicit, ways of extracting, converting, distributing, sharing, using and re-using these two types of knowledge resources. Now, it is time for us to understand the concept of knowledge assets of an organisation.

Knowledge assets are sources within and external to the organisation from which the organisation can gain knowledge and store it for re-use later on. The knowledge assets of any organisation in general can be classified into the following categories:

1. Suppliers

2. Customers
3. Employees
4. Share Holders
5. Public.

Suppliers: The inputs like raw materials, labour and other purchased items going into the product or the service generated by the industry are provided by the suppliers of the organisation. Complete knowledge of the various possibilities in the supplier market gives the organisation strength to produce a better product or generate a better service. Managing supplier information is one of the main tasks of knowledge management in any organisation.

Customers: These are the people who buy the products or services of an organisation. The products and services are designed and manufactured to satisfy the requirements of the customer which constitutes the demand in the market for the specific product or service. In service industries like say, education, health or hospitality and tourism, the customer still rules the roost. Colleges offer degree programmes which are in demand in the job market and required by the employers of the students who pass out of these colleges. The students, hence, would compete to get admission to these courses if they are motivated by their needs to succeed in the job market. Acquiring knowledge with a view to satisfy the customers is part of the responsibility of organisations, regardless of the type they fit in to. Organisations clever in dealing with the customer, changing specifications of the products they manufacture or services they offer from time to time to suit customer demands, invariably stand better chances of succeeding in their stated missions.

Employees: In fact, the main challenge in managing knowledge in a work environment is with regard to tapping the knowledge and skills the average employee possesses and converting them into assets which the organisation can use to its advantage. This is perhaps the key to building an innovative environment which will, later on, translate into competitiveness and improved productivity. Identifying 'knowledge workers', structuring the knowledge environment for content generation and sharing of knowledge, motivation pf people for knowledge sharing are some of the most challenging jobs which many organisations do not pay attention to. A properly structured and knowledge managed organisation will even engage a full time manager to do the job of taking the organisation forward with regard to the specific accumulation, distribution and re-use of knowledge for the betterment of the organisation. A team of specialists working under this Chief Knowledge Officer work constantly towards this purpose. In a later chapter, we will discuss the organisational structure and support system required for effective knowledge management.

Shareholders: Generally, the shareholders, especially the largest ones, participate in the annual general body meetings, when they get opportunities to share their knowledge with other shareholders, small and big. Unfortunately, these meetings end up routine transactions pertaining to finance and other matters, very little time is spared for sharing experiences which can be re-used for the enhancement of knowledge of all concerned which can be converted to improved performance and productivity. What is normally done is to produce brochures containing a lot of information for the benefit of all stake holders describing the visions, missions and goals of the organisation for the ensuing future years with reasons and justifications which becomes the basis of future plans which the shareholders and employees who are also shareholders can relate to. Some of the organisations print and circulate quarterly or bi-annual magazines and journals in which the thoughts of the shareholder-leaders which can involve working and non-working directors, are regularly shared with employees and other shareholders.

Public: The products and services generated by any company or organisation get distributed to the public through the supply chain. The public use the products and services rendered by the firms. Customer support is provided as and when the public face difficulties with the use of the end products and services provided by the firms. The challenge in knowledge management is the ability of the firms to interpret the feedbacks provided by the public into useful, innovative ideas which will improve the products, service applications and tools. This does not generally happen with many firms who believe that they can give ideas to the public, but the public in turn can not contribute to idea generation leading to greater innovation and competitiveness. This myth has to be broken. Greater opportunities for the public to give feedbacks and useful suggestions for product improvement must be made available. Some enlightened firms pay the greatest attention to this aspect namely, receiving feedbacks from the public for product and service improvement. They stand to benefit and gain a competitive edge over the rivals in the long run.

Intellectual Property (Ref. 7)

We have explained the earlier paragraphs that there are four methods of converting knowledge from one form, namely, tacit into another form, namely, explicit. The conversion from tacit to explicit is called articulation while conversion from explicit to tacit is called internalisation. The process of converting knowledge stored in an explicit form to another explicit form or format is called combination.

The explicit documents thus generated, the processes written down and stored as explicit documents and all the knowledge assets of the company registered or patented with a government authority legally, constitute the intellectual property of an organisation. These of course, must be original and not copied from other sources which may be the intellectual property of another organisation or individual.

While we access information from the intellectual properties of others for our use or reference, obviously, a written permission will be required for re-use by us. Any violation of this norm will constitute an illegal act suable in a court of law. Intellectual property disputes are sometimes common even among large corporates.

Intellectual Property Rights

Intellectual property rights include patents, copyright, industrial design rights, trademarks, trade dress, and in some jurisdictions trade secrets. There are also more specialised varieties of *sui generis* exclusive rights, such as circuit design rights (called mask work rights in U.S. law, protected under the Integrated Circuit Topography Act in Canadian law, and in European Union law by Directive 87/54/EEC of 16 December 1986 on the legal protection of topographies of semiconductor products), plant breeders' rights, plant variety rights, industrial design rights, supplementary protection certificates for pharmaceutical products and database rights (in European law).

Patents

A patent is a form of right granted by the government to an inventor, giving the owner the right to exclude others from making, using, selling, offering to sell, and importing an invention for a limited period of time, in exchange for the public disclosure of the invention. An invention is a solution to a specific technological problem, which may be a product or a process.

Copyright

A copyright gives the creator of an original work exclusive rights to it, usually for a limited time. Copyright may apply to a wide range of creative, intellectual, or artistic forms, or "works". Copyright does not cover ideas and information themselves, only the form or manner in which they are expressed.

Industrial Design Rights

An industrial design right protects the visual design of objects that are not purely utilitarian. An industrial design consists of the creation of a shape, configuration or composition of pattern or colour, or combination of pattern and colour in three-dimensional form containing aesthetic value. An industrial design can be a two- or three-dimensional pattern used to produce a product, industrial commodity or handicraft.

Trademarks

A trademark is a recognisable sign, design or expression which distinguishes products or services of a particular trader from the similar products or services of other traders.

Trade dress

Trade dress is a legal term of art that generally refers to characteristics of the visual appearance of a product or its packaging (or even the design of a building) that signify the source of the product to consumers.

Trade secrets

A trade secret is a formula, practice, process, design, instrument, pattern, or compilation of information which is not generally known or reasonably ascertainable, by which a business can obtain an economic advantage over competitors or customers. In the United States, trade secret law is primarily handled at the state level under the Uniform Trade Secrets Act, which most states have adopted, and a federal law, the Economic Espionage Act of 1996 (18 U.S.C. §§ 1831–1839), which makes the theft or misappropriation of a trade secret a federal crime. This law contains two provisions criminalising two sorts of activity. The first, 18 U.S.C. § 1831(a), criminalises the theft of trade secrets to benefit foreign powers. The second, 18 U.S.C. § 1832, criminalises their theft for commercial or economic purposes. (The statutory penalties are different for the two offenses.) Trade secret law varies from country to country.

Objectives of intellectual property law

The stated objective of most intellectual property law (with the exception of trademarks) is to "Promote progress. By exchanging limited exclusive rights for disclosure of inventions and creative works, society and the patentee/copyright owner mutually benefit, and an incentive is created for inventors and authors to create and disclose their work. Some commentators have noted that the objective of intellectual property legislators and those who support its implementation appears to be "absolute protection". "If some intellectual property is desirable because it encourages innovation, they reason, more is better. The thinking is that creators will not have sufficient incentive to invent unless they are legally entitled to capture the full social value of their inventions". This absolute protection or full value view treats intellectual property as another type of "real" property, typically adopting its law and rhetoric. Other recent developments in intellectual property law, such as the America Invents Act, stress international harmonisation.

Financial incentive

These exclusive rights allow owners of intellectual property to benefit from the property they have created, providing a financial incentive for the creation of an investment in intellectual property, and, in case of patents, pay associated research and development costs. Some commentators, such as David Levine and Michele Boldrin, dispute this justification.

In 2013 the United States Patent & Trademark Office approximated that the worth of intellectual property to the U.S. economy is more than US$5 trillion and creates employment for an estimated 18 million American people. The value of intellectual property is considered similarly high in other developed nations, such as those in the European Union. In the UK, IP has become a recognised asset class for use in pension-led funding and other types of business finance. However, in 2013, the UK Intellectual Property Office stated: "There are millions of intangible business assets whose value is either not being leveraged at all, or only being leveraged inadvertently".

Economic growth

The WIPO treaty and several related international agreements underline that the protection of intellectual property rights is essential to maintaining economic growth. The *WIPO Intellectual Property Handbook* gives two reasons for intellectual property laws:

One is to give statutory expression to the moral and economic rights of creators in their creations and the rights of the public in access to those creations. The second is to promote, as a deliberate act of government policy, creativity and the dissemination and application of its results and to encourage fair trading which would contribute to economic and social development.

The Anti-Counterfeiting Trade Agreement (ACTA) states that "effective enforcement of intellectual property rights is critical to sustaining economic growth across all industries and globally".

Economists estimate that two-thirds of the value of large businesses in the United States can be traced to intangible assets. "IP-intensive industries" are estimated to generate 72 per cent more value added (price minus material cost) per employee than "non-IP-intensive industries.

A joint research project of the WIPO and the United Nations University measuring the impact of IP systems on six Asian countries found a positive correlation between the strengthening of the IP system and subsequent economic growth.

Economists have also shown that IP can be a disincentive to innovation when that innovation is drastic. IP makes excludable non-rival intellectual products that were previously non-excludable. This creates economic inefficiency as long as the monopoly is held. A disincentive to direct resources toward innovation can occur when monopoly profits are less than the overall welfare improvement to society. This situation can be seen as one of market failure, and an issue of analysis and correction.

Morality

According to Article 27 of the Universal Declaration of Human Rights, "everyone has the right to the protection of the moral and material interests resulting from any scientific, literary or artistic production of which he is the author". Although the relationship between intellectual property and human rights is a complex one, there are moral arguments for intellectual property.

The arguments that justify intellectual property fall into three major categories. Personality theorists believe intellectual property is an extension of an individual. Some believe that intellectual property stimulates social progress and pushes people to further innovation. Some argue that intellectual property is justified based on deservedness and hard work.

Patent infringement

Patent infringement typically is caused by using or selling a patented invention without permission from the patent holder. The scope of the patented invention or the extent of protection is defined in the claims of the granted patent. There is safe harbour in many jurisdictions to use a patented invention for research. This safe harbour does not exist in the US unless the research is done for purely philosophical purposes, or in order to gather data in order to prepare an application for regulatory approval of a drug. In general, patent infringement cases are handled under civil law (e.g., in the United States) but several jurisdictions incorporate infringement in criminal law also (for example, Argentina, China, France, Japan, Russia, South Korea).

Copyright infringement

Copyright infringement is reproducing, distributing, displaying or performing work, or to make derivative works, without permission from the copyright holder, which is typically a publisher or other business representing or assigned by the work's creator. It is often called "piracy". While copyright is created the instance a work is fixed, generally the copyright holder can only get money damages if the owner registers the copyright. Enforcement of copyright is generally the responsibility of the copyright holder. The ACTA trade agreement, signed in May 2011 by the United States, Japan, Switzerland, and the EU, requires that its parties add criminal penalties, including incarceration and fines, for copyright and trademark infringement, and obligated the parties to active police for infringement. There is a safe harbour to use copyrighted works under the fair use doctrine.

Trademark infringement

Trademark infringement occurs when one party uses a trademark that is identical or confusingly similar to a trademark owned by another party, in relation to products or services which are identical or similar to the products or services of the other party. As with copyright, there are common law rights protecting a trademark, but registering a trademark provides legal advantages for enforcement. Infringement can be addressed by civil litigation and, in several jurisdictions, under criminal law. In the United States, the Trademark Counterfeiting Act of 1984 criminalised the intentional trade in counterfeit goods and services and ACTA amplified the penalties.

Trade secret misappropriation

Trade secret misappropriation is different from violations of other intellectual property laws, since by definition trade secrets are secret, while patents and registered copyrights and trademarks are publicly available. In the United States, trade secrets are protected under state law, and states have nearly universally adopted the Uniform Trade Secrets Act. The United States also has federal law in the form of the Economic Espionage Act of 1996 (18 U.S.C. §§ 1831–1839), which makes the theft or misappropriation of a trade secret a federal crime. This law contains two provisions criminalising two sorts of activity. The first, 18 U.S.C. § 1831(a), criminalises the theft of trade secrets to benefit foreign powers. The second, 18 U.S.C. § 1832, criminalises their theft for commercial or economic purposes. (The statutory penalties are different for the two offenses.) In Commonwealth common law jurisdictions, confidentiality and trade secrets are regarded as an equitable right rather than a property right but penalties for theft are roughly the same as the United States.

References

1. Malhotra, Yogesh. (1998). Knowledge Management, Knowledge Organisations and Knowledge Workers: A View from the Front Lines [WWW document]. URL: http://www. brint. com/interview/maeil. htm
2. Dr Viswanathan Gopalan, 'Knowledge Management, Challenges in the IT Era', ISSN Journal, 2014, ASM Group, Pune.
3. Rebecca O. Barclay, Philip C. Murray, What is knowledge management, http://www. media-access. com/whatis. html
4. David Gurteen, Creating a knowledge sharing culture, February 1999, http://www. gurteen. com
5. Thomas H. Davenport, knowledge management at Ernst & Young, 1997.
6. Tiwana Amrit, the knowledge management toolkit 2th, Prentice Hall PTR 2002.
7. Wikipedia, The Free Encyclopedia, 2014.

Part A
Knowledge Management in Organisations

Chapter 3

Structuring an Organisation for Knowledge Creation and Sharing

"No thief, however skilful, can rob one of knowledge, and that is why knowledge is the best and safest treasure to acquire."

—L. Frank Baum

Knowledge management is a process of transferring new knowledge by creating, classifying, saving, sharing and innovating via technology to deliver to others, then helping organisations or individual to generate a higher real value from document management, core competence management and knowledge community management. Hence, the essence of knowledge management is sharing knowledge with others and make everyone not only become good but also better than before.

Knowledge Creation Cycle (Ref. 3, 4, 8)

Tacit Knowledge

One of the first and most critical points to be looked at in Knowledge Management is that many organisations ignore some of the most important available knowledge in people. Most organisations focus their management on the "explicit" knowledge, the stuff that is easy to explain and write down. But every person has a great deal of "tacit" knowledge they possess but have a hard time explaining or communicating. If you are trying to help someone, but you can't tell them, you can just show them, that is tacit knowledge. Educational systems generally focus on delivering and assessing explicit knowledge. One of the biggest disasters of the downsizing craze was that it was obvious that recent graduates provided more current explicit knowledge at a greatly reduced salary cost. What was invisible until after the downsizing was that the firm ran largely on tacit knowledge of the business and operations, of which the new comers with a lot of knowledge on explicit knowledge had zero contribution. Many businesses found themselves having to hire back the laid off senior people as consultants just to keep the business running.

Knowledge Transformation

So, the biggest challenge in managing knowledge in running businesses is collecting tacit knowledge available in individuals and converting or transforming this tacit knowledge in to explicit forms such as documents and information stored in computers now a days with the advent of technology and make it available to everybody.

The reverse process of distributing explicit, documented knowledge for individuals to read, absorb and share so that it gets embedded in a tacit form in the minds of individuals is part of the challenge too, in knowledge transformation.

In the earlier chapter, we have discussed the meaning of these two processes extensively and hence we will not spend more time discussing the same here.

Knowledge sharing (Ref. 1, 2)

Creating knowledge in a tacit or explicit form or converting it to the other forms is not the only challenge. The equally important challenge is to 'share' knowledge with those around so that it can be used and re-used for the benefit of every one in an organisation. This should eventually lead to greater innovation, productivity and competitiveness is not an academic aspiration of 'Knowledge Champions', but a reality experienced by ardent practitioners of knowledge management. In other words, the benefits far outweigh the costs involved in the long run, though the short-term results are hard to quantify and measure.

There are several steps involved in creating a knowledge sharing culture in an organisation. They are:

1. Identifying knowledge domains to create and share knowledge.
2. Identifying knowledge workers who will create and/or share knowledge.
3. Structuring the organisation for knowledge management efforts.
4. Developing technology platforms and content generation for KM.
5. Implementation of a system for measuring contribution in Knowledge sharing.
6. Rewarding top contributors for knowledge sharing.
7. Organising events to celebrate and commemorate KM.

We will look at each of these steps in the entire process in detail, in the following sections.

Identifying Knowledge Domains

Knowledge is all pervasive and prevalent in all forms in all places and all human minds. This is a fact everyone understands. An automobile industry specialises in the design, manufacture and sale of a car or a truck while a power generation company will be focussing on the generation of power in a specific way, be it thermal or hydraulic or solar energy tapped in a certain way, for generation of electric power. It is quite obvious that even this classification of industries into categories such as automobile, chemical, power, electronic, construction etc., are based on the assumption that one industry cannot master all kinds of knowledge available on planet earth for use and exploitation for business purposes. In each of these huge domains, there can be further classifications. Example, an automobile industry can manufacture a car or a truck, a four wheeler or a two wheeler motor cycle, a petrol or a diesel vehicle, an electric car or an electric-petrol hybrid category. The options are unlimited.

Having identified domains in which knowledge sharing needs to be encouraged, the company must engage itself in the task of structuring itself for practicing knowledge management in an organised way. We will discuss the issue of first identifying people or knowledge workers they are better called who will carry the flag of spreading knowledge awareness, sharing and distribution. Secondly, we will share with you some of the administrative structures preferred to be maintained for the spread and re-use of knowledge for productive, innovative purposes.

Identifying knowledge workers

There may be a large number of knowledgeable people in any organisation. However, a knowledge worker is one who has been identified in various knowledge domains of usefulness and handpicked for the specific job of creating knowledge documents and artifacts, spreading awareness and distributing these assets among the normal employees so that they can re-use the knowledge obtained from these assets and be more productive. Thus, a knowledge worker is a committed expert in specific areas of expertise, willing to spend time in creating, storing and sharing re-usable knowledge with others for the benefit of the organisation. He can be a domain expert or a technical guy willing to work on the technology aspects of building knowledge tools such as data bases, web portals for access, retrieval and storage of information and knowledge or can be an evangelist who goes around talking about KM and creating interest and motivation in people, training them and monitoring the progress made by other employees in sharing knowledge relevant to company working.

Knowledge workers can be further designated as knowledge champions, knowledge reviewers, or knowledge gurus depending on the roles they play. A knowledge champion evangelises the caise of knowledge sharing and management while a reviewer checks often the progress made by the organisation in terms of its usage and a knowledge guru educates, trains and mentors people for the effective use of knowledge management by the company.

Structuring an Organisation for Knowledge Management

Creating a proper structure for administering and implementing knowledge management is very essential because the scope of KM is so vast, the very purpose of it can be lost in a vast sea of information. The organisational objectives may be lost and productivity may take a beating if a proper structure for implementation and control is not instituted, authorities and responsibilities assigned to individuals for managing the efforts and delivering results.

Gencrally, a top level committee is instituted first which is given the responsibility and the authority that goes with it for implementing a structure for KM and proliferating KM practices within the organisation. Under this committee are two separate wings normally, one for generating contents in the form of tacit and explicit knowledge, domain-wise, and the second one for managing the technology resources required for the entire task. In the modern days, this could mean managing computer servers, designing front end portals on the internet to enable the users to log in, insert, store, retrieve, modify and save information.

On the content side, a domain-wise or area-wise creation of knowledge workers, categorised, as discussed earlier, in to knowledge champions, reviewers and gurus, is first accomplished. These knowledge workers go about doing the job of creating knowledge assets which are finally available in explicit formats most of which now-a-days, through the computer, on the internet or intranet. Technology has made access of information and knowledge easy and the task of storage in explicit paper format has become almost redundant in most of the organisations. The documents can always be printed as and when required at will.

Developing Technology Platforms and Content Generation

Like we have mentioned in the previous paragraphs, the most significant tasks in knowledge managing a company or an organisation are:

(a) Content generation –for sharing.

(b) Designing and developing technology platform- for storage and distribution.

Content generation, as we have already mentioned involves the task of converting the tacit knowledge available in the minds of the individuals in to explicit forms like documents, audio and video formats. Converting already available explicit information in to standard formats for storage purposes is also an equally important task. Nowadays, downloading explicit information available on the net without infringing on the copyrights of authors by acknowledging them or taking approval from them is done by many knowledge creators and workers. This is done absolutely within the limits of any intellectual property laws of any nation relevant to the context of storage and sharing of information.

Even books are available on the net. While this cannot be over emphasised, the age old method of buying books and storing in a nice library along with journals, magazines and other manuscripts still remains a popular method of encouraging people to read, learn and gain in knowledge. An organisation, be it an educational entity or a corporate, in the author's opinion is a must for practicing knowledge management seriously. The librarians appointed for this purpose, must be qualified, experienced and dedicated. They can also be called Knowledge Workers of the concerned organisation.

The technology platform for storage, access and distribution has invariably shifted to the computer and the internet in the current era and age. With the advent of computers small in size and large in storage capacity and with the availability of connectivity across all machines in the world through the internet, the task of knowledge sharing has become very easy.

Added to this miracle, is the proliferation of the mobile technology with the new generation mobiles with new connectivity and new applications meant for exchange of explicit documents, videos, pictures and messages. The borders defining the distinction between a phone and computer are vanishing rapidly. One does not know whether another carries a tiny computer or a so called mobile phone in his or her pocket.

So, the author feels that the real challenge is content generation for sharing because, despite the advantage of technology, if the right knowledge is not shared for re-use, the whole concept of knowledge management can easily fail or produce wrong results which will not benefit any one or any organisation.

Measurement of the benefits of implementing KM

The main challenge in measuring benefits of implementing knowledge management in an organisation is that the results are long-term and hence difficult to quantify and measure. Also, if an organisation has performance appraisal systems aimed at rewarding people for their annual work performance in terms of quantity and numbers, the task becomes all the more difficult. To say that a certain amount of innovativeness resulted as a consequence of the presence of the practice of KM is a very difficult logical task. However, the organisations spending money on researching and implementing KM in any reasonable measure, have admitted and research reveals that the long-term benefits in terms of job satisfaction, performance, innovation and competitiveness are many. It is sufficient to say that more research in this area needs to be done so that the benefits of practicing and implementing KM in a work environment can be quantified in measurable units.

Rewarding Contributors in Knowledge Sharing (Ref. 2)

We have discussed elaborately that computers are used to store and retrieve explicit documents to build up the knowledge assets of the organisation. Extending the logistics to store information regarding the identities and other particulars of the employees and the knowledge workers with the details of the documents either generated and stored by them or read only becomes an easy task for the developers of the portals for log in and the servers storing data and information. The types of document, size, confidentiality and importance can be suitably identified in order to allocate points for storage, retrieval, reading and sharing. Lists of people points wise can be pulled out in printed formats to identify and reward contributors.

Having identified top contributors to the challenge of knowledge sharing and proliferation, the reward system can kick in to play. Rewards can be in the form of cash, annual increments, certificates or citations given in public or even redemption of points earned with some established retailers or e-tailers for goods usable by the employees. The author happens to have headed knowledge management initiatives in a company where the annual appraisal allocated 15 points out of 100 for performance evaluation which could lead to increments, bonuses or even promotions. There are companies, especially in the IT arena which go for the system of getting redeemable points converted to useful household and other articles usable by the employee or his family members.

Organising Events to Celebrate or Commemorate Knowledge Management

So, the processes discussed so far in knowledge managing and sharing involve conversion of tacit and explicit information in to explicit knowledge, storage, retrieval and decision of technology mechanisms using IT and software extensively, using the inter and intra net webs, identification of people to do the job of knowledge management, structuring the organisation unit-wise or practice-wise for knowledge propagation and finally instituting a system for recognising and rewarding top contributors.

The last and the most significant step which many organisations do not follow while some enlightened companies do is to celebrate Knowledge Management as a special occasion or an annual day to remember its role, commemorate it as a celebration and highlight its significance. This can be a workshop, a seminar, a conference at the national or even at the international level in the case of companies which are multi-national in character. Eminent Knowledge Gurus, academicians, research scholars, corporate managers and leaders along with the average employee and stake holders can be invited to participate, present papers, talks etc so as to kindle the spirit of knowledge sharing among all present. Magazines, publications and journals, web sites on net can later on highlight the occasion itself by sharing information regarding the event. Excellent effective use knowledge workers can be publicly recognised and rewarded in front of people in order to maintain motivation at a personal as well as organisational level.

The author's opinion as an expert in the field of Knowledge Management is that this single step contributes to the lifting up of the morale and motivation of the stake holders of an organisation to such a level that the KM initiative sustains despite challenges and leads to greater performance, innovation and competitiveness for excellence.

References

1. Malhotra, Yogesh. (1998). Knowledge Management, Knowledge Organisations and Knowledge Workers: A View from the Front Lines [WWW document]. URL: http://www. brint. com/interview/maeil. htm
2. Dr Viswanathan Gopalan, 'Knowledge Management, Challenges in the IT Era', ISSN Journal, 2014, ASM Group, Pune.

3. Rebecca O. Barclay, Philip C. Murray, What is knowledge management, http://www. media-access. com/whatis. html
4. David Gurteen, Creating a knowledge sharing culture, February 1999, http://www. gurteen. com
8. David J. Skyrme, The 3Cs of knowledge Sharing:Culture, Co-operation and Commitment, August 2002 http://www. skyrme. com/updates/ u64_fl. htm

Chapter 4

Knowledge Management Practices in Some Leading Multinational Companies

"For me, I am driven by two main philosophies: know more today about the world than I knew yesterday and lessen the suffering of others. You'd be surprised how far that gets you."

—Neil deGrasse Tyson

We have seen already in the earlier chapters that in the modern day, knowledge management in organisations is very much based on the use of computerised systems for enabling the implementation. So, in this chapter, the author tries to give a bird's eye view of how some of the leading IT companies in the world have tried to structure and implement Knowledge Management in them and the processes they have adopted for effective application.

Before these examples are illustrated, we will discuss some of the issues involved in effective implementation of knowledge management in organisations in general.

What Practices an Organisation Needs to Adopt for Effective Knowledge Management (Ref. 2)

The following are some of the steps involved in implementing knowledge management by any organisation which is serious about the task and wishes to succeed in reaping the benefits out of the challenge. Some of these steps have already been discussed under the topic 'Structuring an Organisation for KM' in Chapter 3 and hence may sound repetitive. However, the list is more elaborate and complete. A brief discussion of all of these issues will lead to a very thorough understanding of the scientific process of implementing knowledge management in any organisation of medium or large capacity.

Identify 'Knowledge Domains'

Identification of domains in which the organisation would focus on is invariably the first task in implementing KM. The areas identified will, in many cases, tally with the departmental or functional areas of production, planning, quality, sales etc. However, the organisation in addition to accumulating, storing and sharing knowledge in these domains, may also decide to focus in more domains such as research, knowledge regarding competitors, their products and services. Thus, many companies do nowadays, without trespassing in to any of the legal boundaries among them. Whenever infringement of any legal nature takes place, litigations are likely to follow. So, care needs to be exercised in accessing information pertaining to competitors. Whatever information is available in the public domain, thanks to the advent of internet technology, can always be used for study, research and comparison which can lead to improved competitiveness and innovation on the part of any company.

Identify 'Knowledge Workers'

This issue has also been discussed in the last chapter. A knowledge worker is different from an ordinary employee in the sense that the knowledge worker is willing to devote extra time, apart from his regular work which his job demands, for activities aimed at institutionalising KM in the company as strategised and planned by the top level committees heading KM initiatives. The knowledge worker does the job of accumulating useful knowledge in tacit and explicit forms and eventually tries to convert all into explicit formats which can be uploaded into knowledge bases or knowledge servers to accessed later on by all the stakeholders through portals designed for accesss, retrieval and sharing using current computer technology.

Depending upon the roles played by each, they can be further classified into knowledge champions, knowledge reviewers, knowledge gurus or knowledge evangelists etc. No one is superior or inferior. One can play more than one role depending on the context and the work volume. Unlike the usual administrative, vertical hierarchies with authority and responsibility we normally encounter in organisations, the KM structures are much more flexible. The following are some of the good practices adopted by some multinational companies who have established Knowledge Management in a fairly elaborate way for the benefit of the company.

- Form 'Knowledge Networks' led by Knowledge Workers.
- Design and Install 'Knowledge Bases'(Repositories) which are technology driven.
- Encourage Stake Holders to 'SHARE' knowledge through the knowledge bases.
- Encourage Stake Holders to 'SHARE' knowledge through Seminars, Workshops, Presentations, Class room Training Programmes etc.
- Train people on 'KM Concepts'.
- Institutionalise Systems for 'Rewarding' and Recognising 'Knowledge Workers' and Other Knowledge people.
- Create Structures and formulate strategies for the above.
- Identify, measure and improve the effectiveness of KM by identifying it with Corporate Objectives and Missions.
- Use KM to foster innovation and to leverage Organisational Wisdom for surviving and coping with competition and changes.

As discussed in the preceding sections, identifying domains and knowledge workers is the most important and prime job. But, equally important is the task of letting enabling them to form networks within the company and outside so that important knowledge pertaining to the products, services and processes can be shared among them. What is generally done is the creation of 'Data Bases' or 'Knowledge Repositories' using latest Information Technology Tools. Once this is done, all the stake holders are encouraged to access these repositories stored in databases in computer servers, and share knowledge. Appropriate front end web portals are designed to provide a user-friendly mechanism to log in and deal with information. Facilities likely, upload, download documents, read share and modify, participate in discussions, knowledge forums on line etc are provided while building these IT applications meant purely for this purpose of knowledge managing the company.

Some of the desirable requirements of good repositories for knowledge sharing are indicated below. The purpose is to provide guidance to any one wishing to introduce knowledge management in any organisation in a scientific way.

Features of a Good IT Knowledge Repository

- Organise and share knowledge.
- Capture knowledge automatically.
- Categorise and classify knowledge assets.
- Find relevant knowledge with simple search.
- Identify and locate knowledge experts.
- Automate knowledge management processes.
- Access websites, intranet and network drives.
- Obtain knowledge with queries.
- Integrate knowledge from multiple repositories.
- Broker searching of legacy search engines.
- Work with popular applications.

- E-mail documents to and fro.
- Document life cycles with records management.

It may not be possible to provide repositories with all the features mentioned above. It is important to provide as many features mentioned above as possible while designing IT applications for the said purpose.

Knowledge Management in Leading Global IT Companies

AAAA (Name not mentioned) Software Systems Ltd

Company Profile

- Global Leader in Services and products for Fixed and mobile networks.
- Started in 1990s with a few persons.
- Today the company has thousands of employees.
- It has offices in several countries including India.
- Represented through its distribution channels in many countries.
- CMMI-Level 4/ISO-9001:2000/BS7799 certified.
- Components of KM System in the above company.
- Time sheet system for activity booking.
- Project Repository.
- Employee Data Base.
- Process data base for accessing HR/Quality and all functional processes. Suggestions for improvement of processes through this mechanism.
- Defect AnalysisWeb System for Causal Analysis.
- Re-use Repository for identifying Re-usable design components.
- Oracle-Based ERP systems.
- Skill Inventory Data Base.

- CRM Tool Repository for collecting and sharing customer related information.

Important KM Practices in the above company

A. Find New Knowledge:

- Tech consultants track knowledge and 'share'.
- The company engages external consultants who are also multinational companies.
- Technical Discussion Groups.
- Several e–discussion groups.

B. Creating New Knowledge

- The company spends 14 per cent of revenues annually on R&D.
- It is a member of technical bodies international in character.
- Its employees publish papers in national/international journals and conferences.
- Central library in addition to group libraries.
- Periodic best practices meet to share knowledge.

C. Packaging/Storing knowledge

- Repositories mentioned earlier.
- An intellectual property management programme spotting innovative ideas and processing them through patent filing.
- Constant on-line communications with stake holders.

D. Applying Existing knowledge

- Transparent work flow application for logging, tracking and closing procedural non-compliances.
- Formal inspection of all artifacts as mandated by the quality system.
- A formal training where buddies and mentors help new engineers do their first project that adheres to company processes.

- Most trainings are conducted by internal faculty.
- Good practices are spread through recognition, awards and internal transfers through Internal job advertisements (IJPP).

E. Reusing Existing Knowledge

- Every project plan identifies re-usable components.
- Central Repository for Training materials.
- Central tool Repository holds User Comments.
- Web Repository for policies and processes.
- Technical paper writing is encouraged in the company.
- Integrated application for easy access of re-usable components.

BBBB(Name not mentioned) Technologies Ltd.

Company Profile

- Founded in India in the 1980s.
- Revenues exceed several Billion rupees.
- The company services fortune 1000 clients in North America, Europe and Asia Pacific.
- Employs a huge number of persons running in to thousands.

The company is considered among India's leading wealth creators.

Deployment of KM initiatives at the company

- Formal KM initiatives born in 1999 when the CEO of the company decided that "Knowledge Sharing" through a common Umbrella is a must for progress.
- Main objective of KM in at BBBB: (1) People, (2) Technology, (3) Process and (4) Content.

The Architecture of the KM set up

- There is a central KM steering committee for Policies and a KM group for implementation.

Incentives for Knowledge Sharing in the above company

- Participation in the acquisition, submission, reviewing and re-use of knowledge tools is the key objective.
- Incentive for this kind of 'knowledge sharing' is mainly through the KCU (Knowledge Currency Units) scheme though it is not limited by it.

KCU Scheme

- Authors earn their KCU when their contents are accepted for publication.
- Users when they find a document useful can award KCUs to authors of docs.
- Subject Matter experts (K Gurus) are also rewarded points through KCUs for the documents reviewed by them.
- KCUs can be converted to Digital Certificates which can be used for making purchases at a specified e-tailer with which Infosys has arrangements for redemption.
- Periodic K-Summits for celebrating Knowledge Sharing activities and to publicly recognise and reward the leaders in Knowledge Sharing.

IT Giant-CCCC(Name not mentioned) – Knowledge Management Journey

Company Profile

- One of World's largest independent SW Companies.
- Annual revenues in Billions of dollars.
- Company offers a range of tools and application products. with consulting, education and support services.
- Operates in over 150 countries in the world.

- Employs over 40,000 people.
- The company offers a full suite of e-business products.
- It offers ERP solutions for enterprises.

Why Knowledge Management in this company?

- "KM increases the exchange of ideas. This turns in to better products, better services, better delivery, more revenue. And asset re-use means repeat revenue and cost savings flowing straight to the bottom line. A no-brainer" says a senior manager of the company.
- The central team consists of 'Change Agents' such as heads of BU or senior managers or consultants.
- The Divisional Teams or the Country Teams consist of Project Mangers, team leaders etc with a KM lead person on top.
- The Central Team is responsible for KM strategies and ensuring that they are aligned with those of the DTs or CTs.

The DTs or CTs have the responsibility of implementing the same at their levels.

Key Components of the Intranet tool used for KM in the said company

Portal and a Repository Framework- for

(1) Web publishing,

(2) Knowledge Sharing,

(3) KM tools to Connect people,

(4) Enable Collaboration, and

(5) Self-service employee applications for day-to-day execution of personal tasks.

Key KM Tools used by this company

(These are complimentary to the portal and repository framework)

- *Seminars*: Used for Webcasts, Application sharing and on-line meetings.
- *Online Forums*: For moderated and archived discussions.
- *Polling and Survey Tools*: To run online polls and comprehensive surveys.

Lessons Learned by Company CCCC- in KM

- Concentrate on issues important to Business.
- KM is not a solution to all problems. It is not positioned as 'A Silver Bullet'.
- KM projects must be short, say six months duration.
- Centrally driven, locally owned KM projects succeed.

Where is CCCC headed in KM journey?

- Involving partners and customers in sharing through I-nets.
- Connecting with theoreticians and practitioners of KM in the world.
- Collaboration with Universities.
- The concept of 'The Learning Organisation', which the company defines as 'A state of being where each individual learns by interacting and sharing their learning with others, causing the organisation to learn'.

HR Practices Encourage Learning and sharing behaviour using professional communities.

The main challenges in implementing KM in any Organisation

- Getting employees to share,
- Letting Technology dominate,
- No specific business goals,

- KM is not a static process-It is Dynamic,
- Making people realise that all info may not be Knowledge,
- Providing 'LEADERSHIP' in KM, and
- Quantifying and Measuring the benefits of KM.

References

1. Dr Viswanathan Gopalan, 'Knowledge Management, Challenges in the IT Era', ISSN Journal, 2014, ASM Group, Pune.

   KM research & Content

Part B

Knowledge Management in People's Lives

Chapter 5

Managing Stress in Life –The Importance of Knowledge

"The possession of knowledge does not kill the sense of wonder and mystery. There is always more mystery."

—Anaïs Nin

One of the most critical challenges people face today is the issue of managing stress and coping with it while striving to compete, achieve and fulfill goals and aspirations in life. The author in his book titled, '*Motivation-The Essence of Living*' has dealt with stress management and its connection with motivation via the process of need identification, goal setting and drive. In this book, the same ideas, in a different form are re-visited, however, from the perspective of the importance of knowledge in coping with stress and living healthily. The author wishes to emphasise that while stress management issues may appear to remain the same, the reader is enabled to look at the significance of focussing on the knowledge required to deal with it and the framework required to do so. The author believes that knowledge, created, interpreted, understood, retained, stored, recalled and re-used in any context, in any form, in any framework finally fits into one entity called 'knowledge' which is all pervading and omnipotent. Read on and enjoy what he tries to share with you. It, sure, will be useful in managing your life more beneficially, even if it does not provide a solution to all the challenges you face in life.

Some General Information on Stress (Ref. 11, 12, 13)

Stress is recognised as the number one killer today. The American Medical Association states that stress is the cause of 80 to 85 per cent of all human illness and disease every week. Ninety five million Americans suffer some kind of stress-related symptom for which they take medication.

American businesses lose an estimated several billion dollars per year to stress-related productivity loss and other cost. To put this in perspective, this amount is higher than the total cost related to all strikes and the net profit from all Fortune 500 companies!

In women, stress has been linked to fatigue, hair loss, bad complexion, insomnia, disruption of the menstrual cycle, low libido and lack of orgasm, among others. Women risk more serious problems such as high blood pressure and heart disease.

Young people grow old faster with stress. Studies reveal that Stress Reduces the Power of your Immune System. Studies show that in women the abdominal fat increases with stress. Stress increases heart rate and blood pressure. It changes the inner lining of our blood vessels, making our blood more likely to clot. Stress may change the way cholesterol is handled by our blood vessels and, in doing so, may increase plaque formation. A study of many pregnant women in Denmark showed that women who are under moderate to high stress in the last stages of pregnancy are 1.2 to 1.75 times more likely to give birth prematurely.

These facts obviously are worth noting and are definitely a cause of our concern, before we decide to face and manage stress in an integrated manner without losing out on life and living.

What is Stress? Definition

(Ref. 11, 12, 13)

- "Stress is the non-specific response of the body to any demands made upon it" – Dr Hans Selye, Father of Stress Studies - 1951.
- "An adaptive response to an external situation that results in physical, psychological, and/or behavioral deviations for organisational participants" – Fred Luthens, Organisational Behavioral Scientist.
- Doctors define that stress is the breakdown of the coping mechanisms of the body and the mind.

Examples of Stress

- Your car about to get involved in an accident- You escape at the last moment.
- Job-related stresses like an unreasonable boss, too much work, unreasonable customer, being passed over for promotion.
- Relationship induced events such as marital problems, death of a spouse, divorce.
- Money-related problems such as not being able to return a loan.
- Health problems such as a serious illness.
- Psychological and emotional problems such as thinking of the results of the examinations expected, a performance appraisal pending, an operation for which you are getting ready—causing a lot of anxiety. The above can trigger sleep induced disorders which in turn causes a 'domino effect' resulting in more stress.
- Self-induced pressures like when you think that you are not performing well and may be fired from your job.
- Conflicts such as choosing between jobs, choosing among partners while planning to get married. Moving to a foreign country leaving friends and families.

Examples of Major Life Events which are stressful and their ranking according to a scientific study

Thomas Holmes and Richard Rahe, developed a list of major life stressors. These are listed in descending order below, beginning with the most stressful event. Only a few in the list are mentioned below, to enable the reader to understand the issue.

1. Death of a spouse, 2. Divorce, 3. Marital separation, 4. Imprisonment, 5. Death of a close relative, 6. Personal injury or illness, 7. Marriage, 8. Fired from a job, 9. Marital reconciliation, 10. Retirement, 11. Illness of a relative, 12. Pregnancy, 13. Sexual problems, 14. Birth or adoption, 15. Business readjustment.

There are many more in the list of Stressful Life Events of Dr Homes and Dr Rahe. All are not mentioned here by the author.

Classification of Stress (Ref B. 10)

Stresses can be classified into the following four categories for clarity in understanding their nature and 'dealing' with them by anyone who faces them and has to cope.

1. *According to Effect*
    1. Positive (Eustress) – "Sukha" in Sanskrit
    2. Negative (Distress) – "Dukkha" in Sanskrit
    3. Neustress – Indifference to Stress
2. *According to Intensity*
    1. Life threatening – e.g. A terminal illness like cancer
    2. Non-life threatening – e.g. An examination
3. *According to Levels*
    1. Extrinsic – At the Organisational level
    2. Intrinsic – At the individual level

4. *According to Source*
   1. Adjustment Stress
   2. Adaptability Stress
   3. Confusion Stress
   4. Conviction Stress
   5. Ego Stress
   6. Situational Stress
   8. Frustration Stress

Sources of Stress –'Stressors' (Ref B. 10)

The following are the most common sources of stress which people encounter in their lives.

(a) Physical – Pollutants, Noise, Cold, Heat (b) Social - Death of a family member, loss of job, fights in family etc. (c) Psychological – Frustration, guilt, worry, fear, self-pity, anxiety etc. (d) Negative "Self-Talk" (e) Chronic negative thinking leads to distress and eventual illness. (f) Hopelessness. This leads to Chronic Depression.

What needs to be appreciated is the fact that once the sources are identified, we can prevent being stressed out by combating the sources rather than the effects of the 'stressor'.

Our Body's Reaction to Stress -General Adaptation Syndrome - (GAS)

1st Stage-Alarm Reaction

A number of chemicals including Adrenaline release, body tenses up, heart beats faster, breathing becomes harder, eyes dilate etc. This is called the 'Fight or Flee' Syndrome. This is done by nature to protect us, if something bad happens. Once the cause of the stress is removed, the body will go back to normal.

2nd Stage-Resistance or Adaptation

If the causes are not removed, more hormones are released causing blood sugar and BP to go up. The adrenal cortex (outer covering) produces hormones called corticosteroids for this resistance reaction. Overuse by the body's defense mechanism in this phase eventually leads to disease. If this adaptation phase continues for a prolonged period of time without periods of relaxation and rest to counterbalance the stress response, sufferers become prone to fatigue, concentration lapses, irritability and lethargy as the effort to sustain arousal slides into negative stress.

3rd Stage: Exhaustion

In this stage, the body has run out of its reserve of body energy and immunity. Mental, physical and emotional resources suffer heavily. The body experiences "adrenal exhaustion". The blood sugar levels decrease as the adrenals become depleted, leading to decreased stress tolerance, progressive mental and physical exhaustion, illness and collapse.

The hypothalamus-pituitary-adrenal (HPA) chain of command has served humans well as a means of survival for thousands of years

However, for those suffering from chronic anxiety and depression this process malfunctions. Continual stress early in life disrupts the cycle. Instead of shutting off once the crisis is over, the process continues, with the hypothalamus continuing to signal the adrenals to produce cortisol. This increased cortisol production exhausts the stress mechanism, leading to fatigue and depression. Cortisol also interferes with serotonin activity, furthering the depressive effect.

Continually high cortisol levels lead to suppression of the immune system through increased production of interleukin-6, an immune-system messenger. This coincides with research findings indicating that stress and depression have a negative effect on the immune system. Reduced immunity makes the body more susceptible to everything from cold and flu to cancer.

Thus, very often, people with prolonged stress may contract diseases related to immune deficiency and may even die of these diseases. The death does not come from stress itself. What happens is that the body loses all its resistance in its effort to ward off the stress. Thus, the persons die of immune deficiency causes such as infection, cancer etc. So, it is very important that we recognise the causes for stresses and remove the causes to maintain a healthy lifestyle.

Warning Signs of Stress (Ref B. 10, B. 11)

Stress is a good teacher. When a person is going through intense stress, the signs appear in the person in various forms such as physical, emotional, cognitive and behavioural. Some examples are given below which are illustrative and not complete.

1. *Physical signs and symptoms of stress-Examples*

Increased heart rate, pounding heart, elevated blood pressure, Sweaty palms, Tightness of the chest, neck, jaw, and back muscles, Headache, Diarrhea, Constipation, Urinary hesitancy, Trembling, Twitching, Stuttering and other speech difficulties.

2. *Emotional signs and symptoms of stress-Examples*

Irritability, Angry outbursts, Hostility, Depression, Jealousy, Restlessness, Withdrawal, Anxiety.

3. *Cognitive/Perceptual Signs and Symptoms of Stress-Examples*

Forgetfulness, Preoccupation, Blocking, Blurred vision, Errors in judging distance, Fantasy life, Reduced creativity, Lack of concentration, Diminished productivity, Lack of attention to detail.

4. *Behavioural Signs and Symptoms of Stress-Examples*

Aggressive behaviours (such as driving - road rage, etc.), Increased alcohol or drug use or smoking, Carelessness, Under eating, Overeating, Withdrawal, Listlessness, Hostility, Accident-proneness. Nervous laughter, Compulsive behaviour and Impatience.

The Effects of Stress on Systems in the Body

It is necessary to understand that stress is affecting us before they become 'chronic' and lead to 'serious health problems' which can sometimes be 'life threatening'. The following section gives a list of 'Health Disorders' or 'Illnesses' which are a result of 'prolonged stresses' in individuals. The list is frightening to the reader, nonetheless, very informative and improves our awareness regarding the seriousness of managing stress without losing health.

Central Nervous System—Anxiety, depression, and fatigue.

Cardiovascular System—Impaired heart function, angina, Constriction of the peripheral blood vessels, blood pressure.

Digestive System—Stomach upsets, ulcers, Diarrhea, Gastritis, and Irritable Bowel Syndrome.

Respiratory System—Asthma.

Musculoskeletal System—Tension in skeletal muscles and joints, backache and muscular aches, pains degenerative diseases like arthritis.

Immune system—Weakened defences, with lowered resistance to infections, Viral illnesses (often due to a depleted immune defence system), Allergies, Cancer.

Endocrine System—Menstrual disorders, Thyroid disorders (underactive, overactive, thyroiditis), adrenal hypo function.

Reproductive System—Infertility, Impotence.

General—Tissue degeneration, Acceleration of aging process

Stress and Performance (Ref B. 10)

Research reveals that performance in a work situation improves up to a certain situation till the stress is enjoyable and positive, called the 'Eustress' and beyond that point when the stress is excessive and distressful, the performance starts waning till it reaches a point of exhaustion and collapse.

Stress at Work Place - Job Stress (Ref B. 10)

Judy Marshall and Cary Cooper have researched on Job Stress immensely. Their findings on the "Sources" of job stress are mentioned below briefly.

- Factors intrinsic to job – Work over load, Too much travel etc.
- Role in the company – Role ambiguity, Role conflict etc.
- Relationships – With the boss, sub-ordinates, peers etc.
- Career development – Stagnation, lack of security etc.
- Organisational Structure and climate – lack of trust, lack of belonging etc.
- Extra-organisational sources – Social Change, Technology Change, family issues etc.

Managing Stress (Ref B. 10, B. 11)

The role of knowledge

The first step in managing or coping with stress is to acquire as much knowledge as possible on the causes of stress and the means to combat them. In the recent times, lot of material is available in explicit form through books, journals, magazines, electronic media including internet. Apart from that, tacit knowledge of stress, fitness and health experts like yoga gurus, body builders and doctors specialising in several areas of health issues is also available though sometimes at an appropriate price dictated by market conditions.

In the following sections, each of these methods of coping with stress and managing it is mentioned briefly while hinting at the importance of knowledge that may have to be specifically acquired in order to achieve the same.

Coping with Stress

Having understood how prolonged stress can damage the body and the mind completely, it is time for us to discuss ways to cope with stress or in other words, 'Manage Stress' so that we stay healthy. There are three ways by which human beings try and cope with stress.

They are:

(1) Defencive coping
(2) Dysfunctional coping
(3) Direct coping.

The following paragraphs explain these methods briefly.

Defencive Coping

The stressed individual uses unconsciously his or her ego-Defence mechanisms which prevent loss of his or her self-esteem.

Examples:

- Denial, Repression, Regression, Projection, Withdrawal, Compromise, Fantacy, Day Dreaming.

Dysfunctional Coping

The affected individual resorts to extreme kinds of behaviour which can be termed 'Dysfunctional'.

Examples such as :

- Maladaptive coping behaviours which lead to increased smoking, too much coffee, alcohol addiction and drug addiction, tendencies to commit suicide.

However, the best way to cope with stress is through Direct-coping discussed in the following sections.

Direct Coping – Positive

The methods suggested below form the crux of 'Stress Management'. The following are the broad classifications.

1. Change your Thinking, 2. Change your Behaviour, 3. Change your Life style, 4. Change from person to a Spiritual person.

They are discussed more elaborately in the following sections of the chapter.

1. Change Your Thinking

Reframing- Positive Thinking

A negative situation may be looked at as an opportunity to learn and hence becomes positive. Example, when a student gets less marks in the exam, he learns that he can do better, works hard ad scores well the next time. People can learn from health problems and improve health, through better diet and exercises and habits.

The reader is encouraged to acquire as much knowledge as possible on the psychology of positive thinking. He or she can read books, listen to talks by experts on positive thinking and put those ideas into practice on a daily basis and learn from them experientially.

Change Your Behaviour

Be Assertive—Learn to say no to negative things and suggestions from others.

Get Organised and do Time Management—Instead of rushing and getting stressed for time, better priority fixing and time management will help ease pressure and tension.

Ventilation—Vent out emotions in a positive way without offending people.

Use of Humour and Laughter—Humour and laughter are the best medicines for health and cheer. Be with people who are cheerful and not those who sulk and complain and look sad.

Diversion and Distraction—While going through difficult situations, think of diverting your attention to positive things to manage stress. During difficult work periods, a week end trip to a holiday resort nearby will help.

Knowledge on behavioural and clinical psychology must be acquired by the reader as much as possible from sources containing explicit information such as books, journals, internet etc., and also listening to talks by experts sharing tacit knowledge gained from their experiences in life through media channels or in person.

Change Your Lifestyle

Diet-Physical Exercise-Relaxation

A good balanced diet rich in protein and vitamins and less in fat, combined with regular exercises like walking, jogging or cycling, playing some active games or workout in a gym with enough rest and relaxation will do the trick of ensuring good physical health and simultaneously a calm mind.

Learning to do simple exercises involving body movements, exercises such as walking, jogging, yogasanas, gym workouts etc. must be learned by the individual and put to use on a regular basis depending on the time available with regard to stress management at one's disposal and one's ability and willingness. Any individual must play atleast one game of his or her choice at regular intervals since it is a great stress buster. Swimming is a great exercise and can be fun and relaxing. It is an all-round exercise for improved health and muscle toning. The author wishes to emphasise, knowledge plus practice of these forms of sports, exercises and games must be acquired and put into useful practice for the overall benefit and health of the individual. It can then be labelled knowledge management with regard to stress instead of calling it just stress management.

Playing with Children

Nothing is more enjoyable in life than playing with small children to bring all the lost qualities in time. Learning from children is part of the challenge. We have to become forgiving and enthusiastic like children to regain our lost motivation to live well.

Knowledge of the behaviour of children, a genuine affection, care and love for children is a must in dealing with children and enjoying their company. Knowledge is acquired through experience and from the others who know a lot about children such as mothers, old people who have reared up generations of children, child psychologists and explicit information available in the form of articles, books and journals on child behaviour. The author is of the opinion from his personal experiences in life that this can be one of the best ways of dealing with stress and learning about the joy of living because, he believes that children are great teachers.

Bio-Feedback

Take feedback from one's own body- mind responses from time to time and adjust the health routines is an advice the author shares with the reader since he has felt the usefulness of this technique through personal experience on a regular basis.

A thorough knowledge of the functions of one's own body and its parts, the connection between the mind and body, knowledge regarding how the body responds to stimuli from the surroundings and gives feedback to the mind and how the mind sends signals to the various organs of the body and controls them, will help any person to utilise knowledge management as a tool for helping body cope with stress which will result in better health and happiness for the individual.

Drink Water

Drinking at least two to three litres of water a day is a must. More than 60 per cent of the human body is water. During the day's routines and exertions especially under stress the body loses a lot of water. If not replaced, the body can suffer with diseases like kidney stones, dryness of the mouth, lack of vital energy for movements and actions required to do work of any kind. An average of two to three litres of water is required by a healthy individual to maintain the fluid balance in the body for healthy living.

Deep Breathing

While tension mounts up, a good deep breath, helps ease the tension. Regular pranayama in the morning or evening improves all the body systems and tones up the entire health.

Various techniques of deep breathing, pranayama taught in yoga must be mastered by the individual for effective application of knowledge to stress management. Guidance by a guru and practice on a daily basis helps the individual to gain experience. This knowledge can be shared or transferred to others either tacitly or explicitly in various forms in various sessions. Deep breathing is, according to the author, a very fast and effective technique for relaxation after a day of strenuous work laden with stress.

Nature Walks-Travel

Nothing helps combat stress like a week-end trip to a nearby hill station or a beach resort. A simple trek in the woods nearby will rejuvenate and bring energy back into you.

Nowadays, knowledge on travel destinations, places of stay, modes of travel, booking tickets to and fro, engaging local travel facilities for sight-seeing etc. have been made easy due to the internet web facilities available at your finger tips. Information, historical records of the places of visit have also been uploaded in websites. This has made knowledge management very easy and comfortable for any average citizen of any country or origin to travel and enjoy the experience of travelling even across different countries across different political and cultural barriers. The author is of the opinion that one should take advantage of this opportunity available to all of us.

Imagery Hydrotherapy

Imagining a nice river or a sea or a waterfall relaxes the mind.

A Warm, Hot Bath

This relaxes the body and mind completely after a hard day at work.

Music Therapy

Listening to good, soothing music or singing oneself is a great stress buster.

Acquiring knowledge on music in various categories such as classical, light music, gazals, western music, rock etc. depending on likings of individuals is an important step in knowledge managing music. On top of that, engaging a teacher and learning music of one's liking and choice is the next step. Many may not be able to afford costly teachers. But, plenty of good, talented, dedicated teachers are available in the market. One can always gain more knowledge on music by being their disciples or students. This should result in better enjoyment of music leading to using it as a tool to manage stress first and eventually to attain happiness, bliss and peace in life. The last choice is to learn music by self using the methodology of listening and imitating the style of good singers or musicians. Any common man does this and in several instances, succeeds in singing good songs of one's wishes bringing happiness and joy to oneself. The author believes music is an easy route to happiness and peace and knowledge on music is an inescapable requirement in order to make music happen in our lives.

Reading

Reading good books before going to bed or during holidays at home is a great way to gain knowledge as well as means to focus the mind and stay calm, relaxed and confident.

The author firmly believes that reading books written by knowledgeable people in any field of expertise is the easiest way to gain knowledge and wisdom in that area. He does not believe that everything meant for learning needs to be, 'reinvented' in order to make learning happen in an individual. In the modern era, in the so called internet age, books and even encyclopedias and dictionaries have been uploaded on the net and are easy to access and read. Facilities are available for downloading and printing the same for payment of moderate charges. Computer technology both hardware, networking as well as software have proliferated across the globe crossing boundaries, making the 'knowledge seeker' very powerful in his search for knowledge leading to wisdom and truth ultimately.

Sleep

Sleeping six to eight hours a day is a must for recharging the body and mind. Too much sleep can make one dull and lethargic.

Meditation and prayer before one goes to bed at night helps him get a good sleep. Reading good books of value or of spirituality before sleep leads to a sound, dream-free sleep. Recollecing negative events of the past including the day and completing or dropping them or in other words letting them slip out of your nagging memory will be a good way to end the working day and slipping into a peaceful slumber. Knowledge on all these psychological, yogic and spiritual techniques must be a goal in seeking knowledge, achieving and re-using for the said purpose.

Yoga and Meditation

The benefits of yoga are acknowledged internationally now. Mixing yoga and meditation with normal forms of exercise in a judicial way without overdoing both is a healthy way to live disease free.

Change from a person into a spiritual person

The latest research on the positive effects of 'spirituality' in the mind, body and the spirit of a person reveals enormous benefits ranging from prevention to complete 'Healing' of dreaded diseases like heart ailments, arthritis, back and joint problems and cancer.

The author believes that regular prayer, reading spiritual literature, listening to enlightened spiritual leaders and gurus should become a way of leading a happy, healthy and peaceful life for any individual. The author is personally experiencing this in his life while he also adopts the direct and positive methods of managing stress discussed in the preceding sections. The TV and Internet Media have made access to 'Spiritual Knowledge' easy nowadays. One has to be careful in choosing good sources to obtain spiritual wisdom which will come only through regular practice of what is taught by a great guru and a lot of 'Self-Inquiry'.

Stress and Motivation (Ref. 9, 10)

The functional methods of coping with stress are known to us now. They are methods like doing exercises, relaxation technique, laughing, playing with children, yoga, meditation, travel, prayer, spirituality and so on as mentioned in the foregoing discussions.

We are going to discuss here as to how we can make all the above coping happen in our lives with regard to stress only if we bring in an awareness that 'Motivation' is again a key attitude we need to maintain in order that we can make the above techniques yield results for us for effective stress management.

Role of Motivation in Stress Management

Any issue related to stress and the technique used to manage stress has to be perceived and brought within the gamut of the motivation paradigm.

An example will help.

Let us say that a person decides that keeping physically fit through exercises is a good way to cope with stress. First of all, he or she has to re-define this situation as a motivational issue by understanding the need involved, the goal or the objective to be reached and the drive or the desire to be sustained till the goal is reached.

So far as physical exercises are concerned, the need in any person is physical fitness, the goal is a strong and a fit, muscular body and the method is regularity I exercise, say four or five times a week, followed by healthy, fat-free food and rest in adequate measure.

Once the need-drive-goal model of the physical exercise issue is understood by the person, it is easier for him or her to relate to the motivational challenge involved in sustaining the habit.

Let us take another example, say meditation with a view to manage stress related issues in daily life. To bring in motivation into the habit of meditation on a daily basis, one has to understand the need to use meditation to achieve the end objective of coping with stress. The need in this method can be perceived as relaxation which is purely a physical or mental comfort or a security need or in the case of a more evolved person to understand self which is an actualisation need. For a third person, it can be a combination of security and actualisation.

People may join group meditational programmes in which case the need to belong to such groups of like-minded individuals also gets merged with the need to relax and to actualise. The goal in this case obviously is health, physical, mental and spiritual. The type of meditation, the duration daily etc., will constitute the path and decide the drive the individual needs to develop in order to make meditation habitual in yielding the end result of coping with stress and leading a more meaningful, joyous life.

In short, the author wishes to tell the reader that while he or she tries to manage stress through the various techniques mentioned in the foregoing paragraphs, it is important that he or she remembers to understand the need-drive-goal issues in the methodology which will improve the effectiveness of coping and the possibility of attaining the end results desired.

An entire chapter has been dedicated in the following pages to teach the reader the core concepts in motivation and bring out the correlation between motivation and knowledge management in a more elaborate way. The reader is also advised to read the book, '*Motivation-The Essence of Living*' written by him and published recently, reference www.gyanbooks.com, for a more thorough and exhaustive knowledge on the subject. Several concepts shared in the next chapter have indeed been transferred as they are and shared from the author's book on motivation. The readers who have read this earlier book on motivation are advised not to feel that this is a repetition. They should understand that the context in which the discussion is being carried out is different, namely, knowledge management in personal lives of individuals.

Conclusion

Many techniques of coping with an managing stress in the context of knowledge management were discussed elaborately in this chapter. The same information is available in the book written by the author on motivation. The dimension which has been added is the awareness regarding the acquisition and use of tacit and explicit knowledge on stress and tips to achieve the same. An integrated approach to health is possible only if a thorough knowledge on stress management is acquired first and put into practice is what the author has tried to tell in this chapter. Sharing of the said knowledge with others, obviously, completes the full cycle of knowledge management of stress. This should lead to the enhancement of health, happiness, peace and joy of not only the reader but those to whom he passes on the knowledge, the author firmly believes. This is the main goal of this book too.

References

1. Dr Viswanathan Gopalan, 'Motivation-The Essence of Living', Gyan Books Pvt Ltd, New Delhi, 2014.
2. Dr Anjali Ghanekar, "Organisational Behaviour, Concepts and Cases", Everest Publishing House, Pune, Eighth Edition, 2002.
3. Dr Viswanathan Gopalan, 'Stress Management and the Science of Living', VIPSAR, Indore, ISSN Journal, 2013 June.
4. Stress Management - Helpguide. org
5. *www. helpguide. org/mental/stress_management_relief_coping. htm*

Chapter 6

Staying Motivated in Life – The Significance of Knowledge and its Management

"People don't care how much you know until they know how much you care." —**Theodore Roosevelt**

Basics of Motivation and its Importance (Ref. 19, 23, 24)

The study of human motivation is of great importance in any theory of management. Man is by nature constantly motivated. He is an organic system. The energy he receives from his surroundings through all his senses is converted to action resulting in behaviour. His behaviour is also governed by the relationships between him and the environment which consists of people. Management involves creation and maintenance of environment for performance in which people can perform and be productive while they maintain or sustain their motivation levels constantly throughout their stay in the concerned work environment and also in their personal lives.

The Motivation Process

Motivation is a six phased process which starts with a need deficiency in an individual and his eventual need fulfillment. The six stages involved in the motivational process are:

(1) Need deficiency.

(2) Search for fulfillment of need.

(3) Goal Definition and goal Directed behaviour.

(4) Evaluation of performance.

(5) Evaluation of rewards and punishments.

(6) Re-evaluation of needs.

Diagrammatically it can be represented by the following model (Fig. 6.1) :

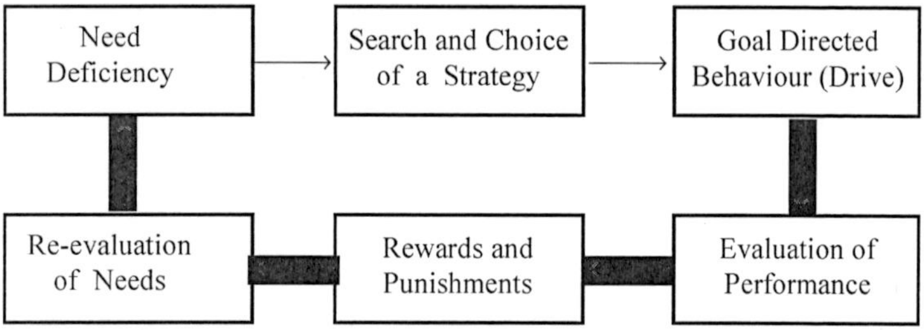

***Fig.* 6.1**

When a person has a need for anything unfulfilled (need deficiency), he searches for ways and means (strategy) to fulfill the need and develops a goal directed behaviour (drive). In that process he obtains results which he evaluates (performance) for satisfaction or dissatisfaction (punishments) and reevaluates his needs for more motivation (the cycle repeats).

The entire process described above constitutes Motivation. The model is applicable to the personal lives of individuals as well as their work lives.

Before we describe the theories of motivation, let us dwell on the definition of motivation for a while.

Definition of Motivation

Webster defines '**motivate**' as to 'provide with a motive', to 'impel', 'incite' and 'motive' as 'that within the individual, rather than without, which incites him to action; any idea, need emotion or organic state that prompts to an action. 'Incite' is also defined as 'to arouse to action, spur or urge on'.

Thus, in order to arouse an individual in to action, it is desirable to determine the motive involved. As this is within the individual, it becomes necessary to study his needs and emotions. It calls definitely for a study of the factors which 'incite' (Incentives) and those which have the opposite effect (Disincentives). Austin defines **disincentive** as that which impedes or tends to impede determination or action. Some popular definitions of motivation are given below.

Definition 1

'Motivation is the result of processes, internal or external to the individual, that arouse enthusiasm and persistence to pursue a certain course of action'.

Definition 2

'Motivation is a process that starts with a physiological or psychological deficiency or need that activates behaviour or a drive that is aimed at a goal or an incentive'.

Importance of Motivation

There are several reasons as to why motivation is vital to an organisational work situation and in the personal life of an individual. The reasons are listed below:

- Motivated people try and do work in ways different from the usual at home and in the work place.
- Motivated people are interested in producing work, which is quality oriented both at home and in a work place.
- Highly motivated people are much more productive than the others. Example: There are several factors attributed to the high levels of productivity in Japan, but motivation is the main factor.

- People must be attracted not only to join an organisation but also must be motivated to stay in it. This implies that an organisation must pay a lot of attention to the motivational environment in a company as well as his personal goals and aspirations.
- In the past the organisations had learnt to look at their technical and financial resources. Only recently, they are learning to give a serious thought to the appropriate use of their human resources. Many organisations are learning to look at their employees as their future resources or "Talent banks". The increasing evidence of this trend is seen in many organisations which are popularising concepts such as "Assessment Center" appraisals, "human resource accounting" etc. More concern is being shown in implementing ideas such as job enrichment, job rotation, training etc. mainly in order to motivate employees so that they become more productive.

Critical Ideas, Terms, Meanings and Concepts in Motivation

The difference between 'Motive' and 'Motivation'

'Motive' can be defined as 'An inner urge that activates, propels or moves the individual towards a 'goal' directed behaviour'.

Some authors distinguish between the words 'needs' and 'motives'. I believe that they can be used interchangeably. The only point I need to mention here is that 'motive' can be a collection of a number of critical needs or can be one dominant single need. However, it is generally a combination of critical needs unsatisfied and need satisfaction either consciously or sub-consciously.

The term 'motivation'on the other hand implies the entire process consisting of need, drive, behaviour, goal attainment, feedback regarding success of goal achievement and continuation of the cycle of motivation. Motive is only a part of motivation but critical to motivation. It is very important and essential.

Motives can be classified into three types.

1. **Primary Motives** – These are physical needs such as hunger, thirst, the need to sleep, sex and so on. These are not learned, but are present physiologically in the individual right from birth.
2. **General Motives** – These are also not learned but are present in individuals as psychological needs such as curiosity, competence, affection, manipulation and so on.
3. **Secondary Motives** – These are learned by the individual during the process of his growth and interaction with society. The need for affiliation, achievement, power, status etc. is learned motives which are prevalent among human beings both in personal lives as well as in their career lives. These motives need to be fulfilled by organisations when they try and motivate employees for greater performance.

These secondary motives are socio-psychological. They are not directly related to survival motives like hunger or thirst. They are learned in a social organisation of any kind. They can further be classified in to (1) Affirmative motive and (2) Egoistic motives. Affirmative motives are positive such as friendliness, kindness, helpfulness, the need to work as a team and so on. Egoistic needs are 'power-centred' such as the need to 'control' others, 'status', money, position and so on. Both these types of motives operate in work environments in deciding the motivation levels of people and hence are very important in studies on motivation.

Behaviour

Behaviour stems from motives. Behaviour is action from motives directed at a 'goal'. The behaviour of an individual may be driven 'consciously' by the individual or sometimes 'sub-consciously. An example may be when an author says he writes a book for contribution as knowledge to society consciously, he may be subconsciously working for name, fame and money. The motives and the goals may vary from individual to individual in a given situation which may appear same or similar which makes motivation a complex phenomenon.

However, it is important for individuals to reflect, understand their conscious and subconscious motives through quiet reflection while pursuing goals or objectives which will fulfil those needs or motives. Otherwise, situations may arise in which the individual turns back and asks the question, "Why did I do it?" or "Why did I not think of it in advance?"

Goals

Goals are specific, outside the individual and achievable. These may be called as 'incentives' by psychologists to motivate the individual. A goal in a work situation may be something as clear as pay, a promotion, a perk like a bonus or a status symbol such as a car, a cabin etc. In personal lives goal can be things clearly achievable like a house, a car, a bank balance, a good wardrobe full of dresses and so on. When we analyse life's issues in the motivational paradigm, it is important to distinguish clearly between needs or motives and goals. Sometimes the individual begins to mix up both. He may think that the need or the motive is what he is seeking. He should set goals clearly and drive himself to reach the goals thus satisfying the needs or motives which drove him to do so.

Theories of Motivation (Ref. 23, 24)

There are several approaches to the study of human motivation and especially motivation in a work place. Broadly speaking, there are two kinds of theories related to work behaviour and motivation in work environments. They are:

(1) *Contemporary theories :*

(a) Maslow's Need Hierarchy Theory

(b) Herzberg's Two Factor Theory

(c) Alderfer's ERG Theory
(d) McClelland's 3n Theory (3 needs)
(e) Manifest Needs Theory
(f) Vroom's Expectancy Model
(g) Adam's Equity Theory
(h) Porter's Performance Satisfaction Theory.

I chose the following "Content" theories, content implying the "Human Need Factor" as the basis for our discussion and the knowledge of the reader. These are the most significant according to me:

(a) Maslow's Need Hierarchy Theory:
(b) Mc Clelland's 3n (Achievement, Affiliation, Power) need theory.

Content Theories

These theories use individual needs to help in the understanding of job satisfaction and work behaviours. Needs reflect physiological or psychological deficiencies. Content theories agree that

Needs → activate → tensions → that influence → Work Behaviour

Stated more clearly content theorists suggest that in order to motivate people, their needs must be assessed and the rewards decided.

Maslow's Need Hierarchy Theory (Ref. 13)

Abraham Harold Maslow is the proponent of his famous theory on motivation based on a "Hierarchy of needs". It is by far the simplest and the best known of all theories on motivation. The essence of the theory can be summarised as follows:

- People are wanting beings whose unsatisfied needs influence their behaviour. The satisfied needs do not motivate while the unsatisfied does.

- There are a number of needs a human being has to cope with and they are arranged in an order of importance (hierarchy) from basic to the most complex.
- A human being advances from one need to another from his basic needs to the more complex, but only when the lower level need of his is fully satisfied.
- As a human being moves further up in his hierarchy of needs, he will display more humanness and psychological maturity and health and will move towards happiness and joy.

The needs : According to Maslow, human needs are grouped into five levels of which the basic level of need comprises of the primary or the physiological ones. The model is illustrated in Fig. 6.2.

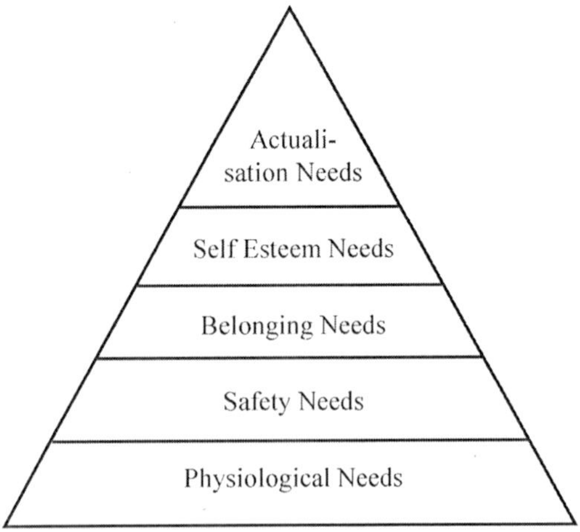

Fig. 6.2

Physiological needs: This is the most basic of all the human needs and the most powerful. Included in this category are needs like the desire for food, thirst, sex, sleep etc. Satisfying these needs are absolutely essential for the human organism to survive.

In other words, the human being will not be around and may perish if these needs are not satisfied for a long period.

Maslow states

For our chronically, extremely, hungry man, Utopia can be simply defined as a place where there is plenty of food. He tends to think that if only he is guaranteed food for the rest of his life, he will probably be happy and will never want anything more. Life itself is defined in terms of eating. Anything else will be defined as unimportant. Freedom, love, community feeling, respect, philosophy may all be waved aside as fripperies that are useless, since they fail to fill the stomach. Such a man may fairly said to live by bread alone (1970).

Security or Safety Needs: Next to the physical needs in the order of priority is the security or the safety need of the person which in essence is more psychological than physical. We deal with factors such as the absence of fear of losing a job and livelihood, fear of living safely and comfortably etc.

Safety needs play a dominant role in a person's life right from childhood. As a person becomes an adult, the needs still dominate. The desire to have a good education, have a secured job with a secured income, the need to have a home with a supportive family etc., are part of this continuing need to have security in life.

Belongingness and Love Need : This constitutes the third level of security in Maslow's hierarchy of needs. The individual affected by this need, longs to be part of a group either in his family or work place. He strives for acceptance into a group either formal or informal. Group membership becomes a dominant goal for the individual. Accordingly, the person may feel the pangs of loneliness or the bliss of 'company'.

Sigmund Freud believed that love meant "Sex" while Maslow said there can be a healthy relationship between two individuals based on mutual trust and affection and love not involving necessarily sex. Maslow was emphatic that the need involves both giving and receiving. Not being loved leads to a feeling of emptiness, hostility and futility.

In the organisational context, this need can exemplify compatible work groups, peer acceptance, professional friendship and friendly supervision.

Self-Esteem Needs: Once the individual satisfies his belonging needs, according to Maslow, he tries to address his self-esteem needs. Maslow has classified these needs into two further subsets: (1) self-respect and (2) respect from others. Self-respect can imply feelings such as confidence, competence, personal strength, adequacy, achievement, independence and freedom. An individual has the right to know that he, as a human being is worthwhile, is capable of contributing and at the same time capable of mastering skills which will enable him to succeed. Esteem from others may include factors such as prestige, recognition, attention, acceptance, status, reputation and appreciation. In this case the individual experience feelings of worth because the others recognise him.

Satisfaction of the self-esteem needs generates feelings and attitudes of self-confidence, usefulness and self-worth, being at harmony with the world. In case these needs are not met with, the individual may feel futile, worthless and hence may feel frustrated and dejected.

The danger of the esteem needs in an individual is that he may begin to rely on others to pass a judgment about his worth exclusively and hence may become very dependent. Others can control him and victimise him into a position of dependency and lack of confidence. In order not to fall a prey to this 'victim' process, the individual has to focus on one's own approval and worth than others worth and others approval.

In a work environment self-esteem needs may correspond to job titles, recognition by others, challenging work, responsibility etc. Managerial practices which can fulfill these needs may include providing employees with challenging work assignments, job enrichment, positive feedbacks on good performance, adding skills through training, recognition through appropriate reward systems, providing a caring, nurturing environment, allowing employees to participate in decision-making and so on.

Self-Actualisation Needs: This indicates, according to Maslow, the desire of the human being to realise one's full potential with regard to certain needs. This can be just as simple as doing work for the sheer joy of it and excelling in it without so much caring about others approval and recognition and focusing so much more on inner satisfaction. People who work at this level have a very high esteem for themselves. They are driven by a "PURPOSE" which is larger than life itself.

Though the need to be self-fulfilled seems very necessary, only a few, the so-called "enlightened" seem to realise it. Maslow himself has estimated that less than one per cent of the population fulfills the need for self-actualisation in the entire world.

Maslow advances three reasons for this happening

(1) People are really not "aware" of their own potentials.

(2) Social environment often stifles the development of an individual.

(3) The most important bottleneck to growth and fulfillment may be the need to be safe. The human being may regress periodically from growing because he may not be willing to take risks. Growing is all about taking risks and the desire to learn.

In an organisational set up, self-actualisation need may manifest in an individual in his need to excel in jobs, the need to come out with ideas and be creative, the desire to create something new which nobody has done before and so on. Managers who encourage people to be creative are specifically enhancing the self-actualisation needs in individuals. Changing, growing organisations must address this need in individuals if they want to benefit from the excellence of a few individuals.

Deficit vs Growth Motivation

Maslow also distinguishes between "Deficiency" and "Growth" needs. Deficiency needs correspond to physical and security needs approximately. Deficiency or D-Needs in an individual imply that if the need is there like starving or dying of thirst, the organism can not "focus" on anything else. Maslow meant by growth needs, the desire to attain happiness which implies the higher level need from belonging to self-actualisation.

Growth needs or Meta needs or B-motives indicate a person's urge to bring out his inborn potentials. Growth needs are not concerned about "tension" reductions as about expansion of mental horizons in order to achieve one's own inner potentials in life.

The Merits and Limitations of the Need Hierarchy Model

First, Maslow's Need Hierarchy theory is by far the most popular of all motivational theories. In fact, we can safely say that there is no one, no manager in an organisation who is not familiar with this theory. Every one identifies himself or herself with this theory that it is easy to recognise these needs in individuals and the organisation can try and satisfy these needs so that the individual fees motivated and so the organisation can hope for more output (productivity) from the individual.

Secondly, Maslow seems to answer questions which have puzzled managers and other individuals in a work place. Sometimes, the management wonders why certain individuals are motivated by money while a few do not care. Maslow's need hierarchy theory supplies the answers for the intra and inter personal variations in behaviour in a given situation in a work place.

Thirdly, Maslow's need model describes human needs and behaviour as a very dynamic activity expressing itself as a constant desire to change for better growth through the process of attainment of unfulfilled higher level needs. The theory states that man or woman does not rest on past glories but moves on restlessly until his or her actualisation potentials are fulfilled which may never be the case in many individuals and hence the world remains an active place.

Fourthly, Maslow was the one to deviate from the early theories on human behaviour proposed by Colossals in the field of psychology such as Freud who believed all behaviour is the result of the sexual needs in individuals. Maslow's beliefs are based on EXISTENTIAL PHILOSOPHY which states that man is a very creative being, different from animals, striving constantly to lead a meaningful life of achievement and finally reach his destined full potential. Maslow must be credited for the positive psychology he introduced in behaviour analysis and modification and hence contributing immensely to the study of motivation.

Lastly, the theory is extremely simple and easy to understand. It is excellent because of its humanness and intuitiveness.

There are several criticisms and limitations to the theory.

1. First and foremost, the hierarchy which Maslow talks about does not exist in practice. All the need of human beings are parallely existing, some dominant and others not so dominant. Another criticism against Maslow's theory is that even if the needs in human beings are hierarchical in order, the need priorities may vary from culture to culture and hence perhaps from country to country. For example, in India, the basic or the physiological needs may be at the bottom of the scale while in a country like America, it may be at the middle of the pyramid of needs. In a country like Japan, social needs may be at the highest level and so on.

2. The same argument may be applicable to differing types of organisational cultures. In a country like India, there are various kinds of organisations like the public sectors, the private sectors, and among the private sector enterprises those run by family controlled organisations like those belonging to some communities, those belonging to some of the affluent families and so on. The need pattern in individuals "adjusted" to the above cultures may be different in these situations.

In spite of all the limitations and criticisms mounted against it Maslow's theory explains best the importance of human needs in a work situation, especially the significance of higher order needs like esteem and actualisation. I strongly felt that even in the current changing scenario in the world of Internet working and global advance in technology, Maslow's need model can explain why people may decide to produce or refrain from it.

The 3N Theory of Achievement, Affiliation and Power by David C. McClelland (Ref. 15)

David C. McClelland and his associates, in 1940, proposed this theory on human motivation which is popularly called the 3n theory, emphasises primarily on the needs of high achievers (nAch) in work places. However, McClelland studied the power (nPow) as well as the affiliation (nAff) of individuals in organisations. Briefly stated the theory is as follows.

Need for achievement(nAch): There are high achievers in work places who achieve tasks quickly and assess themselves for performance and satisfaction. They earn a lot of wealth not for the sake of money per se but with a view to measure themselves with wealth as a yard stick. These persons take moderate and not high levels of risk. They like tasks of reasonable difficulties and dislike easy tasks and easy success. They work independently and like to achieve independently.

McClellend believed that these high achievers can be made role models in industries for others to emulate so that the organisations can become more productive.

Need for power (nPow): Individuals exist in organisations with high need for power and they derive satisfaction from being in positions of power to influence and control others. Organisations, which encourage an authoritative environment, attract individuals with power need and they tend to perform better than others in those places.

Need for Affiliation (nAff): An organisation consists of individuals of this category, who are motivated to have a strong bondage with others for interpersonal ties and to get close to them psychologically. Persons with high affiliation needs tend to choose friends than competent persons in order to work in groups.

Barriers to Motivation

In this chapter, we will introduce to the reader some of the common obstacles and challenges faced by people in a work environment or in personal life which will result in loss of motivation and hence lead to frustration and lack of performance. We are going to show how these obstacles or 'barriers' to motivation can be dealt with and overcome.

The Frustration Model of Motivation

We have understood from the foregoing chapters that motivation consists of a process involving need identification ⟶ Drive ⟶ Goal achievement.

Imagine an obstacle or a barrier being introduced between the drive and the goal portion of this process. What occurs as a result is a phenomenon called frustration for the individual involved I the motivational issue.

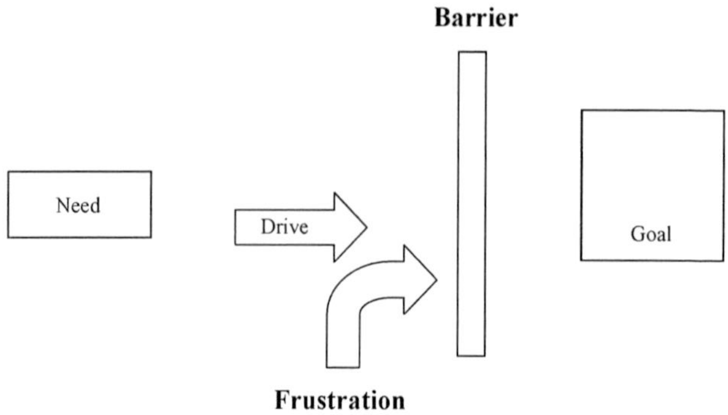

***Fig* 6.3**

Frustration can occur because of the barrier which can be physical like someone physically pulling you away from reaching your goals or psychological of your own making or imposed by those around. We will be focusing in the following paragraphs, on the psychological and socio-psychological barriers detrimental to motivation and some of the means or techniques we can adopt in order to face them, overcome them and stay motivated to reach the set goal.

Psychological, Self-induced Barriers

Self doubts

These can range from uncertainty of understanding the needs, lack of clarity regarding goals, losing drive when difficulties are encountered on the way to achieving a goal, uncertainty regarding one's own ability to sustain the drive and reach the goal and so on.

Lack of Self-esteem

Self-esteem indicates respect for oneself regardless of what others think of you. Even if the skills to achieve a goal or vision is missing, a person with self-esteem will not lose faith in himself, but go on to build the skills without losing heart. So, motivation calls for a lot of self-esteem needs to be satisfied and dealt with in an individual.

Lack of strategies and plans

There are situations in which the needs are clear to the individual and so are the goals and the guy has enough energy and drive. However, he may lack the knowledge and skills to strategise and plan the process of moving forward that after a while he loses direction and control. The net result is the loss of energy and purpose. Despite efforts, the end of the tunnel does not seem to be visible.

Lack of a long-term dream or vision

Some people identify needs; work on short-term goals with drive and enthusiasm. However, they are unable to dream big and sustain the dream for long periods of time. This results in their spending efforts at doing several short-term projects successfully, but they are unable to stay focused on certain long-term, self-discovering initiatives which can give them prolonged happiness and satisfaction. In other words, these people are hard workers and achievers, but lack direction and purpose in life and career.

Social Barriers to Motivation

In many instances, the individual has clear cut needs, sufficient drive and long-term goals defined, but lacks social support, approval and sanctions to carryout the tasks leading to fulfilment of needs and achievement of dreams. The following are some of those issues which the individual needs to be aware of so that he can tide over them wherever they are missing and not feel demotivated and frustrated.

Others do not approve –Approval or Power Need

If you are working for satisfying the needs or sometimes the egos of other people and they do not give that final nod of approval of what you are doing or about to do, there is every possibility that you end up in frustration.

Others do not delegate responsibility and authority -Power Need

In several situations, you are reporting in a structure of hierarchy wherein the people above need to trust you and delegate responsibility commensurate with authority to carryout tasks. The example can be that of a purchase manager in a factory, who is asked to identify a potential supplier of a commodity but not allowed to place an order on the supplier and requires a sanction from his superiors. Another example is that of a housewife who has to take the consent of her earning husband even for the daily purchase of essential goods the household requires. The result of this lack of delegation of power leads to frustration of the individual affected and the consequent demotivation.

Ohers do not consult you – Affiliation Need

You are asked to do and shoulder some responsibility, but others above decide what has to be done or how it has to be done and you are told to do the same without questioning the authority of those who told you to do, can be a very frustrating and annoying situation. This is typical scenario in many work situations and this is a great contributor of all-round frustration of individuals and a cause for demotivation and loss of collective morale. This is a dictatorial way of managing things and a leadership style, according to me, which prevails in many places in many organisations. We need to be aware that such a situation can confront us in any work environment or in our personal life situations too.

Others do not recognise you – Recognition Need

Others know that you have handled responsibility and have carried out the job well, but still refuse to recognise you, not even give a smile or better still the proverbial pat on the back.

They do not praise you in public in front of others nor give you a certification of merit, none whatsoever. The result can be very devastating for you if you do not know how to handle such a situation in work life.

In personal life, an unappreciative husband can kill the enthusiasm of a housewife or a nagging housewife can do it to a loving, caring husband, either way.

Others do not include and respect you-Belonging and Esteem Needs

An environment in which you do not get the respect you deserve as a person with his or her own views and opinions or a place which treats you as alien can really upset you and make you lose all your motivation to be useful and purposeful. People above you, below you or parallel to you in a hierarchical structure in a company may sometimes treat you with disrespect and contempt that you can end up in a pile of self-pity and frustration. In personal life the same thing can happen in family relationships which can lead to quarrels and resulting break in relationships. Family courts in India are loaded with divorce cases where the main cause of the conflicts has been lack of mutual respect between couples.

Others prevent you from achieving-Achievement Need

This is different from others not encouraging you or recognising you for your efforts. This is a situation in which obstacles physical and psychological are put in front of you by your enemies or detractors so that you are incapacitated from fulfilling your missions or objectives. The only way to tackle this situation is to confront your detractors and bring them to books or punish them through the process of law in case they resort to illegal means of preventing you from exercising your democratic free rights as an individual.

I have tried to share with the reader, in the foregoing paragraphs some of the main barriers to motivation. Self-induced barriers like self-doubts, lack of self-esteem, lack of strategies and plans, lack of drive and vision are some of the hurdles while social barriers like approval and recognition by others, lack of authority and responsibility to fulfill aspirations in situations where one is dependent on others are factors affecting motivation. In extreme cases, one may have to fight battles to remove obstacles deliberately introduced by others to prevent you from achieving your goals, missions and dreams or visions in life. The key is to think positive, stay positive and motivated in all circumstances and say no to any barrier which comes in the way of staying happy and motivated while you continue to make progress in achieving your life's missions.

Motivation in Personal Life (Ref. 23)

In the following paragraphs, I wish to share with the reader some of the most important tips regarding making motivation work for every individual on a daily basis, but also will result in the achievement of his or her long-term goals and visions as well.

Going back to the models on motivation which I described for the reader in the earlier sections, I would say three elements stand out distinctly in the realisation and achievement of motivation in any one's life. They are:

1. Identification of one's inner needs.
2. Setting up a goal to achieve the result.
3. Developing a plan and maintaining a 'Drive' during the process.

We are going to discuss these three processes in detail in the following sections.

Identifying one's own inner needs

In fact, while a person develops a desire to do or achieve anything, in many cases, he is unable to understand what drives him to do so. He is unable to connect his yearning for a specific object of desire to the core of a burning need in him. This is one of the reasons which prevents people from sustaining the desire when the obstacles come and frustration sets in.

Many people react when asked the question "Why do you do it?, with an immediately answer. "Money". They do not realise that money is not a need, but a means of transacting values. We require money to buy an object like a house or a car. We, in that instance, are addressing our need to buy a house or a car, which could be a physical security need or a status need to be accepted as an important person in society. It can be the esteem and worth need of an individual and in some cases, buying the house may be the ultimate dream or vision of a person in life in which case it tends towards actualisation. Without making this discussion complicated, I wish to point out that while developing ambitions to achieve, one should become need aware.

When an athlete achieves a medal in the Olympics, he or she could be doing for the honour of the country or merely for the sake of enhancing one's own reputation or both in which case the needs of actualisation and self-esteem combined in that individual in the process of achieving the medal and the honours that go with it.

To be brief, the first step in the motivational issues in individual aspirations for achievement is identifying the inner need of an individual, which causes the drive to take place. One should be able to pin point the need clearly as one that belongs to the variety of needs discussed in the various theories on motivation, see, identify and internalise.

Goal Setting

Having identified one's own needs, the next step is to set a clear goal or a set of goals for achievement of an objective. This is like saying, "I am thirsty" or my need is "Thirst" and so my goal is to drink "Water". Then you run around for water, find it, drink it with happiness, quench your thirst and end up satisfied till the thirst occurs again.

The most important considerations in setting goals are;

1. Goals must be specific and achievable.
2. Goals can be achieved within set time limits.
3. Goals must be real and not illusory.

In the example of one drinking water, water can be replaced by other liquids like a fruit juice or coconut water, but cannot be replaced by a harmful acid which may enhance the thirst and simultaneously ruin the liver. Time limits are preferable, else, people may tend to procrastinate and not achieve ever. Some of the searches for a specific goal such as a "Good Guru" or "A true friend" may take longer durations of time than one plans for.

When I say goals must be realistic and not illusory, I mean you cannot set goals like "I want to be the ruler of the world". Set a goal like "I need to be the governor of this district" which is specific and achievable.

Developing a Plan and Sustaining a Drive

The final important step in the motivational process is to develop a strategy or a long-term plan to achieve the mission and break it into achievable short-term objectives or goals and set the action plans on from day one. Slowly but steadily the advance begins and the goals are reached and passed by till the final one arrives which will also eventually come to pass. But the point is that the dream, the vision or the mission gets fulfilled yielding satisfaction and happiness to the individual concerned, leaving him more motivated to achieve other dreams in future.

The biggest challenge in the above process is of course the possibility of 'losing the drive' on the way. It is quite possible the path is filled with blocks to the objective of reaching the goal and frustrations occur as a result. One can 'backslide' and reach a point where progress becomes a lot more difficult.

On those occasions, one has to muster courage, sustain drive and motivation and move on steadily till the final goal is reached. It is all part of the 'big challenge'.

The following are some tips which will enable the common person to practice motivation easily on a daily basis.

Seven Simple Rules of Staying Motivated

1. Set a major goal, but follows a path

The path has mini goals that go in many directions. When you learn to succeed in achieving mini goals, you will be motivated to challenge grand goals which will lead you to the ultimate goal in your vision.

2. Finish what you start

A half-finished project is of no use to anyone. Quitting is a habit. Develop the habit of finishing self-motivated projects. Perseverance and patience are traits that one must cultivate in order to succeed.

3. Socialise with others of similar interests

Mutual support is motivating. We will develop the attitudes of our best friends. If they are losers, we will be a looser. If they are winners, we will be a winner. So choosing the right friends who have positive attitudes towards life in general is a quality one must develop in order to stay motivated and succeed in doing things.

4. Learn how to learn

Dependency on others for knowledge is a slow time consuming processes. Man has the ability to learn without instructors. In fact, when we learn the art of self-education we will find, if not create, opportunity to find success beyond our wildest dreams. Of course now-a-days technology available on the internet enables one to self-learn very fast without having the necessity to go to classes to study.

5. Harmonise natural talent with interest that motivates

Natural talent creates motivation, motivation creates persistence and persistence gets the job done. So, identifying one's own natural talents and nurturing them goes a long way in practicing motivation to do things well.

6. Increase knowledge of subjects that inspire

The more we know about a subject, the more we want to learn about it. We get into a positive cycle of self upliftment that can take us to great heights of achievement and success in the long run.

7. Take risks

Failure and bouncing back are parts of normal living and indeed the key components of motivation. Failure is a learning tool. No one has ever succeeded at anything worthwhile without a string of failures. Great people like Abraham Lincoln are Scientists like Thomas Alva Edison are examples. Take calculated risks and keep learning from failures in order that the lessons can be moulded to pave the way for future success.

The significance and application of knowledge management techniques in Motivation:

1. The first and the most significant step in staying motivated in personal or even professional life is to realise that a thorough knowledge of the motivation process is required by the individual. This will involve a deep understanding of the need-drive-goal-feedback model we discussed at the beginning of this chapter.
2. Understanding and knowing the various types of need that exist in human beings ranging from basic to actualisation according to Maslow's hierarchical model and achievement-affiliation-power model of McClellend is the next step. Introspecting and connecting to one's

own needs classified the above way at every situation and becoming comfortable and aware is an important step in the process of knowledge managing motivation.

3. This is followed by the process of setting visions and missions for long-term strategies of achievement and goals for short-term achievements on the way, during the subsequent journey.
4. The long-term visions are set by the individual after really knowing the most dominant needs in oneself and developing and acquiring knowledge to fulfil the same through dedication, commitment and application. The short-term goals, the plans and the strategies follow smoothly.
5. Acquiring all the tacit and explicit knowledge required to draw this road map for oneself in motivation calls for a lot of effort and intelligence. Practical experience counts a lot while learning from experience and ability to set goals for future ad achieve them matters all the more.
6. Re-use and re-application of knowledge gained during the entire journey constitutes a key component for the success of the process of staying motivated right through. It is quite possible that one 'back slides' when frustrations are encountered. So, it is important to manage frustrations and this may call for a variety of knowledge in stress management as well as psychological and even spiritual tools for coping, managing and succeeding at the end. The main focus should be on acquiring, saving, using and re-using knowledge to combat the challenges of staying motivated in life during various challenging situations and come out victoriously.
7. The author wishes to conclude by saying that knowledge and its management is the key for motivation in personal and professional life too.

References

1. A.H. Maslow, "Motivation and Personality", Harper & Bros, New York, 1954.
2. D. C. McClellend, "The Achieving", D. Nostrandco. Inc, Princeton, N. J., 1961.
3. Frederick Hertzberg, Bernard Mausner & Barbara Shydermann, "The Motivation to Work", 2nd Edition, John Wiley and Son. Inc, New York, 1959.
4. Keith Davis and J. W. Newstrom, "Human Behaviour at Work-Organisational Behaviour", Mcgraw-Hill, New York, 1989.
5. Fred Luthens, "Organisational Behaviour", Mcgraw-Hill Inc., New York, 1995.
6. Dr Anjali Ghanekar, "Organisational Behaviour, Concepts and Cases", Everest Publishing House, Pune, Eighth Edition, 2002.
7. David C. McClellend, "Managing Motivation to expand Human Freedom", American Psychologist, 1978.
8. Fred Luthens and Robert Krietner, "The Management of Behavioural Contingencies", Personnel, July 1974.
9. Frederick Hertzberg, "One More Time, How do you Motivate Employees", Harvard Business Review, Selected Articles, Reprint, Motivation, 1970.
10. Dr Viswanathan Gopalan, "Motivation-The Essence of Living" Gyan Books Pvt Ltd, New Delhi, 2014.
11. Dr Viswanathan Gopalan, "Motivation and Its Relevance to Productivity". Thesis for Ph. D, Pune University, 2001.
12. Dr Viswanathan Gopalan, "Motivating Knowledeg Worker". ISSN-Journal Symbiosis, 2012.
13. Dr Viswanathan Gopalan, "The Significance of Motivation with regard to Productivity", ISSN Journal, Amity University, Lucknow, 2014.

Chapter 7

Higher Needs in Life- A Knowledge Management Perspective

"The eye through which I see God is the same eye through which God sees me; my eye and God's eye are one eye, one seeing, one knowing, one love." **—Meister Eckhart**

In the earlier chapters we dealt with the definition and meaning of knowledge, knowledge management and its relevance in professional life, its implementation in corporate houses and businesses, importance in personal life with regard to issues like stress and motivation. In this chapter, we are going to discuss the significance of managing knowledge in the context of the most important, higher level needs and issues in life. The author has thought it fit to delve into four critical issues haunting human beings in their daily lives, even though there are many more issues of significance which need to be resolved. The importance to look at these critical four needs or issues or better still the challenges from a knowledge perspective, the author believes, will enable the reader to understand, know more, use, reuse this knowledge and eventually benefit in life. The human needs considered for analysis and discussion in the knowledge management context are:

1. Love
2. Happiness

3. Peace
4. Spirituality and Enlightenment.

The author wishes to emphasise the fact that under each of these topics, some of the views on these issues from various religions have also been briefly mentioned. The author has researched on previously available material from reliable sources such as Wikipedia and downloaded information which are valid, non-offending and useful. If, however, the reader encounters information which is not to his taste, he is requested to ignore it and move forward, because the intention of the author in sharing all of this knowledge is to enrich and enhance the quality of life of every individual reader and the society.

The next and the last chapter has been entirely devoted to the discussion of 'Spirituality and Enlightenment' while in this chapter an attempt to discuss the other three issues namely, love, happiness and peace in human lives.

Knowledge Management Perspective

Factors Considered

The factors on each of the four above areas of challenge facing mankind which are considered for analysis as well as interpretation from a knowledge management perspective are listed below. This splitting enables the reader to look at the issues from a very rational point of view without losing focus due to emotional clouding which can impede full understanding. The parameters or factors we have looked at are the following:

1. Sources of knowledge.
2. Type of knowledge- Tacit or explicit.
3. Storage – The forms of storage.
4. Issues of use and re-use.
5. Sharing for usefulness and benefit.
6. Quantification of benefits.

The opinions or personal views of the author are interspersed with those views already available on the subject. Appropriate references and acknowledgements have been made wherever necessary. Eventually, how much the reader has gained in terms of knowledge and how much he or she can use them in their personal lives for purposeful living is left to the individual. The author hopes to achieve this objective by sharing, as much his knowledge as possible, on the subject, for reading and assimilation, for use and reuse in life. Let us begin by analysing and understanding each of these first three issues in life, mentioned above, from a knowledge management point of view, one by one.

The Ultimate Purposes, Needs or Challenges in Human Life-KM perspective (Ref. 7)

1. Love

Love is a variety of different feelings, states, and attitudes that ranges from interpersonal affection to pleasure. It can refer to an emotion of a strong attraction and personal attachment. It can also be a virtue representing human kindness, compassion, and affection. It may also describe compassionate and affectionate actions towards other humans, one's self or animals.

Ancient Greeks identified four forms of love:

- kinship
- friendship
- sexual
- self-emptying or divine love

Modern authors have distinguished further varieties of romantic love. Non-Western traditions have also distinguished variants or symbioses of these states. This diversity of uses and meanings combined with the complexity of the feelings involved makes love unusually difficult to consistently define, compared to other emotional states.

Love in its various forms acts as a major facilitator of interpersonal relationships owing to its central psychological importance, Love may be understood as a function to keep human beings together against menaces and to facilitate the continuation of the species.

Definition of Love

Although the nature or essence of love is a subject of frequent debate, different aspects of the word can be clarified by determining what love is not. Love is a general expression of positive sentiment, a stronger form of the word like. Love is commonly contrasted with hate. Love is a less sexual and is a more emotionally intimate form of romantic attachment. Love is commonly contrasted with lust. Love is sometimes contrasted with friendship, although the word love is often applied to close friendships.

Abstractly discussed love usually refers to an experience one person feels for another. Love often involves caring for or identifying with a person or thing. In addition to cross-cultural differences in understanding love, ideas about love have also changed greatly over time.

Impersonal love

A person can be said to love an object, principle, or goal to which he or she is committed. People can also "love" material objects, animals, or activities if they invest themselves in bonding or otherwise identifying with those things.

Interpersonal love is most closely associated with interpersonal relationships. Such love might exist between family members, friends, and couples. There are also a number of psychological disorders related to love.

Throughout history, philosophy and religion have done the most speculation on the phenomenon of love. In the twentieth century, the science of psychology has researched a great deal on the subject.

Biological basis

Biological models of sex tend to view love as a mammalian drive, much like hunger or thirst. Helen Fisher, a leading expert in the topic of love, divides the experience of love into three partly overlapping stages.

1. Lust
2. Attraction
3. Attachment.

Lust is the feeling of sexual desire; romantic attraction determines what partners find attractive and pursue, conserving time and energy by choosing. Attachment involves sharing a home, parental duties, mutual defence, and feelings of safety and security. Lust is the initial passionate sexual desire that promotes mating, and involves the increased release of chemicals such as testosterone and estrogen. These effects rarely last more than a few weeks or months.

Attraction is the more individualised and romantic desire for a specific candidate for mating, which develops out of lust as commitment to an individual mate forms. Recent studies in neuroscience have indicated that as people fall in love, the brain consistently releases a certain set of chemicals, including the neurotransmitter hormones, dopamine, norepinephrine, and serotonin, the same compounds released by amphetamine, stimulating the brain's pleasure centre and leading to side effects such as increased heart rate, loss of appetite and sleep, and an intense feeling of excitement. Research has indicated that this stage generally lasts from one and a half to three years.

Since the lust and attraction stages are both considered temporary, a third stage is needed to account for long-term relationships. Attachment is the bonding that promotes relationships lasting for many years and even decades. Attachment is generally based on commitments such as marriage and children, or on mutual friendship based on things like shared interests. It has been linked to higher levels of the chemicals oxytocin and vasopressin to a greater degree than short-term relationships have.

Psychological basis

Psychology depicts love as a cognitive and social phenomenon. Psychologist Robert Sternberg formulated a triangular theory of love and argued that love has three different components: intimacy, commitment, and passion.

Intimacy is a form in which two people share confidences and various details of their personal lives, as is usually shown in friendships and romantic love affairs.

Commitment, on the other hand, is the expectation that the relationship is permanent.

The last and most common form of love is sexual attraction and passion. Passionate love is shown in infatuation as well as romantic love. All forms of love are viewed as varying combinations of these three components. Lastly, consummate love includes all three.

Psychologist Erich Fromm maintained that love is not merely a feeling but is also actions, and that in fact, the "feeling" of love is superficial in comparison to one's commitment to love via a series of loving actions over time. In this sense, Fromm held that love is ultimately not a feeling at all, but rather is a commitment to, and adherence to, loving actions towards another, oneself, or many others, over a sustained duration.

Evolutionary basis

Evolutionary psychology has attempted to provide various reasons for love as a survival tool. Humans are dependent on parental help for a large portion of their lifespans compared to other mammals. Love has therefore been seen as a mechanism to promote parental support of children for this extended time period.

Religious views

Christianity

The Christian understanding is that love comes from God. Christians believe that to *Love God with all your heart, mind, and strength* and *Love your neighbour as yourself* are the two most important things in life. Saint Augustine summarised this when he wrote "*Love God, and do as thou wilt.*"

The Apostle Paul glorified love as the most important virtue of all. Describing love in the famous poetic interpretation in Corinthians, he wrote, "Love is patient, love is kind. It does not envy, it does not boast, it is not proud. It is not rude, it is not self-seeking, it is not easily angered, it keeps no record of wrongs. Love does not delight in evil but rejoices with the truth. It always protects, always trusts, always hopes, and always perseveres."

In Christianity, the practical definition of love is best summarised by St. Thomas Aquinas, who defined love as "to will the good of another," or to desire for another to succeed. This is the explanation of the Christian need to love others, including their enemies.

Judaism

The commandment to love other people is given in the Torah, which states, "Love your neighbour like yourself". The Torah's commandment to love God "with all your heart, with all your soul and with all your might" is taken by the Mishnah (a central text of the Jewish oral law) to refer to good deeds, willingness to sacrifice one's life rather than commit certain serious transgressions, willingness to sacrifice all of one's possessions, and being grateful to the Lord despite adversity.

Islam

Love encompasses the Islamic view of life as universal brotherhood that applies to all who hold faith. The Qur'an exhorts Muslim believers to treat all people, those who have not persecuted them, with deep kindness.

Ishq, or divine love, is the emphasis of Sufism in the Islamic tradition. Practitioners of Sufism believe that love is a projection of the essence of God to the universe. Since everything is a reflection of God, the school of Sufism practices to see the beauty inside the apparently ugly. Sufism is often referred to as the religion of love. A common viewpoint of Sufism is that through love, humankind can get back to its inherent purity and grace.

Buddhism

In Buddhism, *Kâma* is sensuous love. It is an obstacle on the path to enlightenment, since it is selfish. *Karunâ* is compassion and mercy, which reduces the suffering of others. It is complementary to wisdom and is necessary for enlightenment. *Advec a* and *mettâ* are benevolent love. This love is unconditional and requires considerable self-acceptance. This is quite different from ordinary love, which is usually about attachment and which rarely occurs without self-interest. Instead, in Buddhism it refers to detachment and unselfish interest in others' welfare.

Hinduism

In Hinduism, *kâma* is pleasurable, sensual love, personified by the god Kamadeva. In contrast to *kâma*, *prema* refers to elevated love. *Karuna* is compassion and mercy, which impels one to help reduce the suffering of others. *Bhakti* is a Sanskrit term, meaning "loving devotion to the supreme God." A person who practices *bhakti* is called a *bhakta*.

In certain sects within Hinduism, attaining unadulterated, unconditional and incessant love for Godhead is considered the foremost goal of life.

In the Bhakti tradition within Hinduism, it is believed that execution of devotional service to God leads to the development of Love for God, and as love for God increases in the heart, the more one becomes free from material contamination. Being perfectly in love with God makes one perfectly free from material aspirations. And this is the ultimate way of salvation or liberation.

Love in relationships – Modern view-Author's perspective

Love is expressed as an action and experienced as a feeling. Yet, love has an essence that resists defining in any single way — it encompasses compassion, determination, tolerance, endurance, support, faith, and much more. If you're in the dark about how to love, the following paragraphs should give you some food for thought, and perhaps teach you a little bit about how to love yourself, love the world, and love other people just a little bit more. The author would like to share some thoughts on making relations work in the context of love.

Commitment

If you're in love, prove it by putting effort into the relationship and working hard to make it work. Communicate openly with your partner about your goals for the relationship and where you see it going. If you're only interested in a short-term fling, be honest. If you've got an eye toward serious long-term love, be honest. There's nothing wrong with either kind of love, but you need to make sure that your partner is equally committed to the same version of love that you are. In other words, integrity, transparency and honesty are the key factors apart from commitment.

Commit to the person and to the relationship. It is easy when two people have been together for a while and you've become very trusting to just get very comfortable with each other. Maybe you don't go out on dates anymore or maybe you don't dress up nice for each other sometimes. But you should at least do these things occasionally, or eventually someone will feel like they're no longer worth the effort.

Learning lessons and applying them to your relationships

Unforeseen things may sometimes happen in your relationships. You'll say the wrong thing, or others hurt your feelings. It happens. The important part, when anything goes wrong, is to learn your lessons and just keep moving forward. Try to make the most of any negative situation, turning it into something positive by gaining and growing from the experience. Do try to be compassionate and understand where the experiences are coming from. If you're in the wrong, apologize and own up to your mistake. Good relationships grow when people air out the grievances and clear the misunderstandings. In bad relationships people hide the negativity and let it fester into serious problems. If you're in love, talk about your problems without disrespecting or offending the other. The problems will wither away eventually. It is as simple as that.

Working constantly to make yourself and those you love better and improved

A good, loving relationship is one where people constantly challenge each other to be better people. Help the other person to achieve their dreams and goals because you believe they deserve it. Improve yourself and work for your dreams so that you can be the person you feel you deserve to be. We should be better people because of the relationships that we have, and this is the way to do it.

Eliminating jealousy

This is one of the unhealthiest things to have in relationships, as it can break down trust and respect, and create barriers. For some people, this can be the most challenging part of any relationship. Jealousy is a tough thing to break, but you can do it. The most important thing to understand is that jealousy issues almost always come from within, from the jealous person's own issues, so those need to be worked through first. This is a place where those communication skills come in handy. This is, of course, assuming one person in the relationship is running around blatantlycheating the other. In which case, they don't really love the person they're hurting. Relationships should be based on trust, honesty and commitment as we discussed earlier.

Viewing issues from all sides

We hate to be wrong. All of us do not wish to be wrong. But the thing about everyone thinking they are right is that someone has to be wrong. If we disagree on an issue, we're bound to be wrong on at least part of the issue. We will have much stronger relationships if we learn to talk things out with the other person, see their point of view, and find somewhere in the middle a position where we can meet and agree. If we have trouble agreeing on how we feel about something or someone, let us try to stick first with the facts — some facts maybe have been omitted due to our preferences which really ought to be considered, in all fairness.

Being partners in life

The whole purpose of going through life with people you love is that you can tackle life's challenges together. Work together to find solutions, solve problems, and comforts each other when times get tough. We cannot solve every problem on our own, we cannot know everything there is to know. But, a whole group of people getting together out of love can solve just about any issue.

Happiness (Ref. 7)

Happiness is a mental or emotional state of well-being defined by positive or pleasant emotions ranging from contentment to intense joy. A variety of biological, psychological, religious, and philosophical approaches have tried hard to define happiness and identify its sources. The United Nations declared 20 March the International Day of Happiness to recognise happiness and wellbeing as universal goals.

Definition of Happiness

Philosophers and religious thinkers often define happiness in terms of living a good life, or flourishing life, rather than simply as an emotion. Happiness in this sense was used to translate the Greek Eudaimonia, and is still used in virtue ethics. There has been a transition over time from emphasis on the happiness of virtue to the virtue of happiness.

Happiness can mean many different things to many people. Part of the challenge of the science of happiness is to identify different concepts of happiness, and where applicable, split them into their components. Related concepts are well-being, quality of life and nourishing state of life. One author defines happiness as contentment. Some commentators say that focusing on the differences between avoiding unpleasant experiences, and of living life in a full and a deeply satisfying way makes one understand happiness.

Research results

Since the 1960s, happiness research has been conducted in a wide variety of scientific disciplines. During the past two decades, however, the field of happiness studies has expanded drastically in terms of scientific publications. Research has produced many different views on causes of happiness, and on factors that correlate with happiness, but no validated method has been found to substantially improve long-term happiness in a meaningful way for most people.

It has been argued that money cannot effectively "buy" much happiness unless it is used in certain ways. Beyond the point at which people have enough to comfortably feed, clothe, and house themselves, having more money - even a lot more money - makes them only a little more happier. A Harvard Business School study found that "spending money on others actually makes us happier than spending it on ourselves."

Meditation has been found to lead to high activity in the brain's left prefrontal cortex, which in turn has been found to correlate with happiness.

Humans seem happiest when they have:

1. *Pleasure* (tasty food, warm baths, etc.),
2. *Engagement* (or flow, the absorption of an enjoyed yet challenging activity),
3. *Relationships* (social ties have turned out to be extremely reliable indicator of happiness),
4. *Meaning* (a perceived quest or belonging to something bigger), and
5. *Accomplishments* (having realised tangible goals).

Abraham Harold Maslow, an American professor of psychology, founded humanistic psychology in the 1930s. A visual aid he created to explain his theory, which he called the hierarchy of needs, is a pyramid depicting the levels of human needs, psychological, and physical. When a human being ascends the steps of the pyramid, he reaches self-actualisation. Beyond the routine of needs fulfillment, Maslow envisioned moments of extraordinary experience, known as peak experiences, profound moments of love, understanding, happiness, or rapture, during which a person feels more whole, alive, self-sufficient, and yet a part of the world. Self-determination theory relates intrinsic motivation to three needs: competence, autonomy, and relatedness.

Happiness and religion

There are a number of mechanisms through which religion may make a person happier, including social contact and support that result from religious pursuits, the mental activity that comes with optimism and volunteering. It may also be that religious people engage in behaviours related to good health, such as no-substance abuse, since the use of psychotropic substances is sometimes considered abuse.

The *Handbook of Religion and Health* describes a survey by Feigelman (1992) that examined happiness in Americans who have given up religion, in which it was found that there was relationship between religious disaffiliation and unhappinesss. Repeated findings of research on the science of happiness indicate that there is a positive link between religious engagement and wellbeing. People who report that God is very important in their lives are on an average more satisfied with their lives, after accounting for their income, age and other individual characteristics.

A review of 498 studies published in peer-reviewed journals concluded that a large majority of them showed a positive correlation between religious commitment and higher levels of perceived well-being and self-esteem and lower levels of hypertension, depression, and clinical delinquency. An analysis of 34 recent studies published between 1990 and 2001 found that religiosity has a salutary relationship with psychological adjustment, being related to less psychological distress, more life satisfaction, and better self-actualisation.

Various Religious views on happiness

The Author wishes to emphasise that the following material is not his own, but researched and obtained mainly from documents and references such as Wikipedia and shared with the reader with regard to the positive views of religions on happiness which will be beneficial to him or her to face challenges in life, which is the essence of knowledge management. The author believes that none of the knowledge shared here is meant to hurt any religious sentiments or views of any one.

The author appeals to the reader that mistakes made in references or presentation may be excused and forgiven. The positive thoughts shared may be remembered and re-used in keeping with the spirit of knowledge sharing.

Buddhism

Happiness and peace forms the central theme of Buddhist teachings. For ultimate freedom from suffering, the Noble Eightfold Path leads its practitioner to Nirvana, a state of everlasting peace. Ultimate happiness is only achieved by overcoming craving in all forms. More mundane forms of happiness, such as acquiring wealth and maintaining good friendships, are also recognised as worthy goals for lay people. Buddhism also encourages the generation of loving kindness and compassion, the desire for the happiness and welfare of all beings.

Judaism

Happiness in Judaism is considered an important element in the service of God. The biblical verse "worship The Lord with gladness, come before him with joyful songs," stresses joy in the service of God. A popular teaching by Rabbi Nachman urges people to always be in a state of happiness. When people are happy they are much more capable of serving God and going about their daily activities better than when being depressed or upset.

Philosophical views

In the *Nicomachean Ethics*, written in 350 BCE, Aristotle stated that happiness is the only thing that humans desire for its own sake, unlike riches, honour, health or friendship. He observed that men sought riches, or honour, or health not only for their own sake but also in order to be happy. Note that "happiness", is for Aristotle an activity rather than an emotion or a state. Thus, understood, the happy life is the good life, that is, a life in which a person fulfills human nature in an excellent way. Specifically, Aristotle argues that the good life is the life of excellent rational activity. He arrives at this claim with the Function Argument. Basically, if it's right, every living thing has a function, that which it uniquely does. For humans, Aristotle contends, our function is to reason, since it is that alone that we uniquely do. And performing one's function well, or excellently, is for one's good. Thus, the life of excellent rational activity is happy life according to Aristotle, one of the greatest philosophers human history has produced so far.

Economic views

Some economists claim that economic freedom correlates strongly with happiness, preferably within the context of a Western mixed economy, with free press and a democracy. It has been argued that happiness measures could be used not as a replacement for more traditional measures, but as a supplement.

It has also been argued that happiness at work is one of the driving forces behind positive outcomes at work, increased productivity, motivation and morale, improved relationships between management and workers leading to greater harmony and peace.

Happiness Indices for measurement

Several scales have been used to quantify, compare and measure happiness. Some, below have been indicated by the author, to the reader, for the sake of completion in knowledge on the topic. These measures are:

1. The Subjective Happiness Scale (SHS) is a four-item scale, measuring global subjective happiness. The scale requires participants to use absolute ratings to characterise themselves as happy or unhappy individuals, as well as it asks to what extent they identify themselves with descriptions of happy and unhappy individuals.
   - The Positive and Negative Affect Schedule (PANAS) is used to detect the relation between personality

traits and positive or negative affects at this moment, today, the past few days, the past week, the past few weeks, the past year, and generally (on an average). PANAS is a 20-item questionnaire, which uses a five-point Likert scale (1 = very slightly or not at all, 5 = extremely). A longer version with additional affect scales is available in a manual.

- The Satisfaction With Life Scale (SWLS) is a global cognitive assessment of life satisfaction. The SWLS requires a person to use a seven-item scale to state their agreement or disagreement (1 = strongly disagree, 4 = neither agree nor disagree, 7 = strongly agree) with five statements about their life.

The UK began to measure national well-being in 2012, following Bhutan which had already measured its gross national happiness.

Health and Happiness –Some research information

At University College London researchers collected health and well-being data from 116 men and 100 women. All 216 participants were middle-aged, British civil servants between the ages of 45 and 59. Researchers at the college furthered their studies by using their participants three years later to repeat the physiological measurements. They found that participants who scored high in positive emotion continued to have lower levels of cortisol and fibrinogen, as well as a lower heart rate.

Some studies on happiness and health report that happy people live 14 per cent longer, increasing longevity 7.5 to 10 years.

Happiness at work

There has been a large collection of positive psychologial research work into the relationship between happiness and productivity. Happiness at work has traditionally been seen as a potential by-product of positive outcomes at work.

The Author in his extensive research on motivation and productivity in work places and in personal life, and his book, '*Motivation-The Essence of Living*' has indicated that human needs like recognition, self-esteem and affiliation, when satisfied in work situations lead to improved motivation, morale and happiness, resulting in improved productivity and hence an alround prosperity for the human beings in that environment.

Peace (Ref. 7)

Meaning

Peace is a period of harmony between different social groups. Peace is characterised by lack of violence, conflict behaviours and the freedom from fear of violence. Commonly understood as the absence of hostility and retribution, peace also suggests sincere attempts at reconciliation, the existence of healthy or newly healed interpersonal or international relationships, prosperity in matters of social or economic welfare, the establishment of equality, and a working political order that serves the true interests of all.

The term 'peace' originates most recently from the Anglo-French *pes,* and the Old French *pais*, meaning "peace, reconciliation, silence, agreement" But, *Pes* itself comes from the Latin *pax*, meaning "peace, compact, agreement, treaty of peace, tranquility, absence of hostility, harmony." The English word came into use as a translation of the Hebrew word *shalom*, which comes from a Hebrew verb meaning 'to restore'. At a personal level, peaceful behaviours are kind, considerate, respectful, just, and tolerant of others' beliefs and behaviours, tending to goodwill and happiness.

The understanding of peace can also pertain to an individual's introspective sense or concept of her/himself, as in being "at peace" in one's own mind. The early English term is also used in the sense of "quietness" reflecting calm, serene, and meditative approaches to family or group relationships that avoid quarreling and seek tranquility, an absence of disturbance or agitation.

Religious beliefs and peace

Religious beliefs often seek to identify and address the basic problems of human life, including the conflicts between, among, and within persons and societies.

Many Christians call Jesus of Nazareth the "Prince of Peace", and see him as a 'Messiah', which means Anointed One, the "Christ", who manifested as the Son of God on Earth to establish God's Kingdom of Peace, wherein people, societies, and all of creation are to be healed of evil.

Buddhists believe that peace can be attained once all suffering ends. They regard all suffering as stemming from cravings in the extreme, greed, aversions or delusions. To eliminate such suffering and achieve personal peace, followers in the path of the Buddha adhere to a set of teachings called the Four Noble Truths a central tenet in Buddhist philosophy.

Hinduism

"May there be peace in the heavens, peace in the atmosphere, peace on the earth. Let there be coolness in the water, healing in the herbs and peace radiating from the trees. Let there be harmony in the planets and in the stars, and perfection in eternal knowledge. May everything in the universe be at peace. Let peace pervade everywhere, at all times. May I experience that peace within my own heart." -Yajur Veda.

"A superior being does not render evil for evil. This is a maxim one should observe...One should never harm the wicked or the good or even animals meriting death. A noble soul will exercise compassion even towards those who enjoy injuring others or cruel deeds...Who is without fault?" - *Ramayana* of Valmiki.

The chariot that leads to victory is of another kind. Valour and fortitude are its wheels, truthfulness and virtuous conduct are its banner, strength, discretion, self-restraint and benevolence are its four horses, harnessed with the cords of forgiveness, compassion and equanimity. Whoever has this righteous chariot, has no enemy to conquer anywhere. —*Ramayana* of Valmiki.

Inner peace

Inner peace or peace of mind refers to a state of being mentally and spiritually at peace, with enough knowledge and understanding to keep oneself strong in the face of discord or stress. Being "at peace" is considered by many to be healthy and the opposite of being stressed or anxious. Peace of mind is generally associated with bliss and happiness.

Peace of mind, serenity, and calmness are descriptions of a disposition free from the effects of stress. In some cultures, inner peace is considered a state of consciousness or enlightenment that may be cultivated by various forms of training, such as prayer and meditation.

Satyagraha

Satyagraha is a philosophy and practice of non-violent resistance developed by Mohandas Karamchand Gandhi also known as "Mahatma" Gandhi. He deployed satyagraha techniques in campaigns for Indian independence and also during his earlier struggles in South Africa. This word is commonly translated as 'steadfastness in the truth'.

Satyagraha theory also influenced Martin Luther King, Jr. during the campaigns he led on civil rights movement in the United States. The theory of satyagraha sees means and ends as inseparable. Therefore, it is contradictory to try to use violence to obtain peace. As Gandhi wrote, "They say, 'means are, after all, means. I would say, 'means are, after all, everything'. As the means so the end".

A contemporary quote attributed to Gandhi, sums it up. 'There is no way to peace. Peace is the way.'

Justice and injustice

Discussion of peace is at times is a discussion on the form of such peace. Is it simple absence of mass organised killing (war) or does peace require a particular morality and justice, which we may call 'Just Peace'.

A peace must be seen at least in two forms:

- A simple silence of arms, absence of war.
- Absence of war but accompanied by particular requirements for the mutual settlement of relations, which are characterised by terms as justice, mutual respect, respect for law and goodwill.

More recently, advocates for radical reform in justice systems have called for a public policy adoption of non-punitive, non-violent restorative justice methods, and many of those studying the success of these methods, including a United Nations working group on Restorative Justice, have attempted to re-define justice in terms related to peace.

Organisations for World Peace

United Nations

The United Nations (UN) is an international organisation whose stated aims are to facilitate cooperation in international law, international security, economic development, social progress, human rights, and achieving world peace. The UN was founded in 1945 after World War II to replace the League of Nations, to stop wars between countries, and to provide a platform for dialogue.

The UN, after approval by the Security Council, sends peacekeepers to regions where armed conflict has recently ceased or paused to enforce the terms of peace agreements and to discourage combatants from resuming hostilities. Since the UN does not maintain its own military, peacekeeping forces are voluntarily provided by member states of the UN. The forces, also called the "Blue Helmets", who enforce UN accords are awarded United Nations Medals, which are considered international decorations instead of military decorations. The peacekeeping force as a whole received the Nobel Peace Prize in 1988.

Olympic Games and Peace

The late nineteenth century idealist advocacy of peace which led to the creation of the Nobel Peace Prize, the Rhodes Scholarships, the Carnegie Endowment for International Peace, and ultimately the League of Nations, also saw the re-emergence of the ancient Olympic ideal. Led by Pierre de Coubertin, this culminated in the holding in 1896 of the first of the modern Olympic Games.

Nobel Peace Prize

The highest honour awarded to a peace-maker is the Nobel Prize in Peace, awarded since 1901 by the Norwegian Nobel Committee. It is awarded annually to internationally notable persons following the creation of the prize in the will of Alfred Nobel. According to Nobel's will, the Peace Prize shall be awarded to the person

"Who shall have done the most or the best work for fraternity between nations, for the abolition or reduction of standing armies and for the holding and promotion of peace congresses."

Rhodes Scholarships and other fellowships

In creating the Rhodes Scholarships for outstanding students from the United States, Germany and much of the British Empire, Cecil Rhodes wrote in 1901 that 'the object is that an understanding between the three great powers will render war impossible and educational relations make the strongest tie'.

This peace purpose of the Rhodes Scholarships was very prominent in the first half of the twentieth century, and became prominent again in recent years under Warden of the Rhodes House Donald Markwell, a historian of thought about the causes of war and peace. This vision greatly influenced Senator J. William Fulbright in the goal of the Fulbright fellowships to promote international understanding and peace, and has guided many other international fellowship programmes.

Gandhi Peace Prize

The International Gandhi Peace Prize, named after Mahatma Gandhi, is awarded annually by the Government of India. It is launched as a tribute to the ideals espoused by Gandhi in 1995 on the occasion of the 125th anniversary of his birth. This is an annual award given to individuals and institutions for their contributions towards social, economic and political transformation through non-violence and other Gandhian methods. The award carries Rs 10 million in cash, convertible in any currency in the world, a plaque and a citation. It is open to all persons regardless of nationality, race, creed or sex.

Measuring and ranking peace

Although peace is widely perceived as something intangible, various organisations have been making efforts to quantify and measure it. The Global Peace Index produced by the Institute for Economics and Peace is a known effort to evaluate peacefulness in countries based on 22 indicators of the presence or absence of violence. The last edition of the Index ranks 162 countries on their internal and external levels of peace. According to the 2013 Global Peace Index, Iceland is the most peaceful country in the world while Afghanistan is the least peaceful one.

The Failed State Index created by the Fund for Peace focuses on risk for instability or violence in 178 nations. This index measures how fragile a state is by 12 indicators and sub-indicators that evaluate aspects of politics, social economy, and military facets in countries. The 2014 Failed State Index reports that the most fragile nation is South Sudan, and the least fragile one is Finland.

University of Maryland publishes the Peace and Conflict Instability Ledger in order to measure peace. It grades 163 countries with five indicators, and pays the most attention to risk of political instability or armed conflict over a three-year period. The most recent ledger shows that the most peaceful country is Slovenia on the contrary, Afghanistan is the most conflicted nation.

Besides those measures indicated above, other organisations like the Economist Intelligence Unit and George Mason University release indexes that rank countries in terms of peacefulness.

Conclusion- Love, Happiness, Peace- The Knowledge Management Connection

From all the information that we have presented above on the critical challenges in life, namely, love, happiness and peace, a few conclusions we can arrive at, which we can term as knowledge, which are re-usable and sharable with others for our benefit. Hence, we can use the term 'Knowledge Management' with regard to these challenges confronting our lives. The conclusions, by the author, are briefly presented to the reader, as follows:

1. The definitions, meanings and common perceptions of the concepts of love, happiness and peace have remained the same regardless of time.
2. All religions, communities, cultures and nations have understood the concepts in exactly the same manner even though the means for attainment might have changed here and there. The visions, goals and objectives have been the same across the ocean of humanity spanning ages.

3. The knowledge on these concepts have been shared in olden times as well as the modern era tacitly and explicitly. Tacitly in olden times through teachings and preachings by Gurus, saints and learned men while in the modern era by modern teachers, gurus, saints and thinkers. Explicitly, in olden times, texts and scriptures were used to convey ideas, while in modern times texts, scriptures and story books are compounded by technologies such as the internet, smart phones, TV and other electronic media devices. The objectives of knowledge propagation have not changed with regard to the exchange and interchange of ideas on love, peace and happiness.
4. The author advises the reader to acquire more knowledge on these topics from all available sources in tacit and explicit forms, store in mind, in devices, interpret, analyse, re-use, re-learn, share and mutually benefit for love, peace, happiness and collective welfare.

References

1. Wikipedia, The Free Encyclopedia, 2014.
2. http://www. psychologies. co. uk/love/can-you-learn-to-love-anyone.
3. http://www. eharmony. com/dating-advice/dating/common-love-myths-and-how-they-affect-your-dating-life/#. Ul65gJlDv2lhttp://www. marcandangel. com/2012/06/13/15-relationship-truths-for-tough-times/ http://www. eharmony. com/dating-advice/relationships/eight-valuable-love-lessons-you-need-to-know/#. Ul65fZlDv2l
3. *'Does God exist? Here are six straightforward reasons to believe that God is really there.'* By Marilyn Adamson.
4. R.E.D. Clark, *Creation* (London: Tyndale Press, 1946), p. 20 The Wonders of God's Creation, Moody Institute of Science (Chicago, IL).
5. Hugh Davson, *Physiology of the Eye,* 5th ed (New York: McGraw Hill, 1991).
6. Robert Jastrow, "Message from Professor Robert Jastrow"; *LeaderU. com;* 2002.

7. Steven Weinberg; *The First Three Minutes: A Modern View of the Origin of the Universe;* (Basic Books, 1998).
8. Dinesh D'Souza, *What's So Great about Christianity;* (Regnery Publishing, Inc, 2007, chapter 11).
9. Richard Feynman, *The Meaning of It All: Thoughts of a Citizen-Scientist* (New York: Basic Books, 1998), 43.

Chapter 8

Spirituality- Enlightenment-The Purpose of Life- The Knowledge Connection

"Prayer is not asking. It is a longing of the soul. It is daily admission of one's weakness. It is better in prayer to have a heart without words than words without a heart."

—Mahatma Gandhi

When we begin to move away from the lower level needs of the body and the mind and crave to understand the purpose of life, we are getting in to the realm of spirituality. We are longing to get answers to questions posed by our inner voices like, 'Who am I?', 'Am I the body and mind or is there something beyond, a spiritual form of energy, the soul driving us through our intellect to act in ways that we are yet to comprehend?'. We ask ourselves questions like, 'Why do we suffer despite achievements, the possessions and the wealth we accumulate around us?'. We are constantly tormented by the fear of death, the pain and indignity we may face during the process of death, leaving all our possessions we strive to accumulate. We are afraid of leaving behind the so-called close relations and friends, alone and dying on a lonely hospital bed.

We seek and strive to get answers to important questions such as:

1. What is the purpose of life?
2. Is there anything called eternal happiness or bliss?
3. Can we achieve complete peace and unlimited happiness in this life of ours?
4. Is there life after death?
5. Did we have a past life?
6. Who created the cosmos and the world?
7. Who is God? Is he a person or a spirit?
8. If we, the souls are part of His creation, Is He different from us?
9. How do we attain liberation and freedom from the bondage of life and death?

The author, in the following sections, provides knowledge to the reader which may enable him to understand and possibly get answers to the questions which normally haunt the human mind and perception. From a purely knowledge management perspective, the aim is not to provide answers but to initiate self-reflection and introspection in the individual seeking enlightenment who can choose to follow his own mind and instincts to pursue the quest further.

Let us begin with some of the concepts in spirituality and the terms used in various cultures and religions to enable us to acquire knowledge and hopefully some wisdom in the process.

Enlightenment (Ref. 7)

Enlightenment refers to the "full comprehension of a situation". It is also used in a religious context. It translates several Buddhist terms and concepts like 'Bodhi', 'Kensho', 'Satori' etc., Related terms from Asian religions are Moksha (liberation) in Hinduism, Kevala Jnana in Jainism and Ushta in Zoroastrianism. In Christianity, the word "enlightenment" is rarely used, except to refer to the Age of Enlightenment and its influence on Christianity. Roughly equivalent terms in Christianity may be illumination or revelation.

Buddhism

The English term "enlightenment" has commonly been used to translate several Sanskrit, Pali, Chinese and Japanese terms and concepts, especially *bodhi*, *prajna*, *kensho*, *satori* and buddhahood.

Bodhi is a Theravada term. It literally means "awakening" and "understanding". Someone who is awakened has gained insight into the workings of the mind which keeps us imprisoned in craving, suffering and rebirth, and has also gained insight into the way that leads to *nirvana*, the liberation of oneself from this imprisonment.

In Zen, *kensho* means "seeing into one's true nature". *Satori* is often used interchangeably with *kensho*, but refers to the *experience* of *kensho*.

Buddhahood is the attainment of full awakening and becoming a Buddha, the ultimate goal of Buddhist practice, attained when all limitations have been removed from the mind and one's positive potential has been completely and perfectly realised. It is a state characterised by infinite compassion, wisdom and skill.

Hinduism

In Indian religions, s*moksha* (*mukti* -Sanskrit) means 'release' "to let loose, let go". It represents the final extrication of the soul or consciousness (*purusha*) from *samsara* and the bringing to an end all the suffering involved in being subjected to the cycle of repeated death and rebirth (reincarnation).

Advaita Vedanta

Advaita Vedanta is a philosophical concept where followers seek liberation and release by recognising identity of the

Self (Atman) and the Whole (Brahman) through long preparation and training, usually under the guidance of a guru, that involves efforts such as knowledge of scriptures, renunciation of worldly activities, and inducement of direct identity experiences. Originating in India before 788 AD, Advaita Vedanta is widely considered the most influential and most dominant sub-school of the Vedânta (literally, *end or the goal of the Vedas*) School of Hindu Philosophy.

The key source texts for all schools of Vedânta are the canonical texts consisting of the Upanishads, the Bhagavad Gita and the Brahma Sutras. The first person to explicitly consolidate the principles of Advaita Vedanta was Shankara Bhagavadpada while the first historical proponent was Gaudapada, the guru of Shankara's guru Govinda Bhagavadpada.

Philosophical system

Shankara systematised the works of preceding philosophers. His system of Vedanta introduced the method of scholarly scripts on the accepted metaphysics of the Upanishads. This style was adopted by all the later Vedanta schools.

Neo-Vedanta

In the nineteenth century Vivekananda played a major role in the revival of Hinduism and the spread of Advaita Vedanta to the West via the Ramakrishna Mission. His interpretation of Advaita Vedanta has been called "Neo-Vedanta".

In a talk on "The absolute and manifestation" given at London in 1896 Swami Vivekananda shared the following knowledge and wisdom of his with the world outside, explicitly.

Vivekananda emphasised samadhi as a means to attain liberation. For Shankara, meditation and Nirvikalpa Samadhi are means to gain knowledge of the already existing unity of Brahman and Atman, not the highest goal itself.

Yoga

Yoga is a meditative exercise of withdrawal from the particular and identification with the universal, leading to contemplation of oneself as the most universal, namely, Consciousness.

The prime means to reach *moksha* is through the practice of yoga. *Yoga* is a commonly known generic term for physical, mental, and spiritual disciplines which originated in ancient India. Specifically, yoga is one of the six schools of Hindu philosophy based on the *Yoga Sûtras of Patañjali*. Various traditions of yoga are found in Hinduism, Buddhism, Jainism and Sikhism. While the *Yoga Sutras* focus on discipline of the mind, Hatha yoga concentrates on health and purity of the body.

Hindu monks, beginning with Swami Vivekananda, brought yoga to the West in the late nineteenth century. In the 1980s, yoga became popular as a physical system of health exercises across the Western world. Many studies have tried to determine the effectiveness of yoga as a complementary intervention for cancer, schizophrenia, asthma and heart patients. In a national survey, long-term yoga practitioners in the United States reported musculo–skeletal and mental health improvements.

Jnana yoga

Classical Advaita Vedanta emphasises the path of *jnana yoga*, a progression of study and training to attain *moksha*. It consists of four stages:

Samanyasa or *Sampatti*s, the "fourfold discipline".

Nityânitya vastu viveka — The ability (*viveka*) to correctly discriminate between the eternal (*nitya*) substance (*Brahman*) and the substance that is transitory existence (*anitya*).

Virâga — The renunciation (*virâga*) of enjoyments of objects.

Mumukc utva — The firm conviction that the nature of the world is misery and the intense longing for *moksha* (release from the cycle of births and deaths).

Bhakti yoga

The paths of *bhakti yoga* and *karma yoga* are subsidiary.

In bhakti yoga, the practice centres on the worship God in any way and in any form, like Krishna. Adi Shankara himself was a proponent of devotional worship or *Bhakti.* But Adi Shankara taught that while Vedic sacrifices, *puja* and devotional worship can lead one in the direction of *jnana* (true knowledge), they cannot lead one directly to *moksha.* At best, they can serve as means to obtain *moksha.*

Karma yoga

Karma yoga is the way of doing our duties, in disregard of personal gains or losses.

According to a saint, 'Karma Yoga is consecration of all actions and their fruits unto the Lord. Karma Yoga is performance of actions dwelling in union with the Divine, removing attachment and remaining balanced ever in success and failure'.

'Karma Yoga is selfless service unto humanity. Karma Yoga is the Yoga of action which purifies the heart and prepares the heart and the mind for the reception of Divine Light or attainment of Knowledge of the Self. The important point is that you will have to serve humanity without any attachment or egoism.'

Jainism

Jainism is an Indian religion that prescribes a path of non-violence towards all living beings. Its philosophy and practice emphasise the necessity of self-effort to move the soul towards the divine consciousness and liberation. The ultimate status of these perfect souls is called *siddha.*

In Jainism the highest form of pure knowledge is that a soul can attain what is called Kevala Jnana, which means "absolute or perfect" and Jñâna, which means "knowledge". Kevala is the state of isolation of the jîva from the ajîva attained through ascetic practices which burn off one's karmic residues, releasing one from bondage to the cycle of death and rebirth. Mahavira, 24th thirthankara of Jainism, is said to have practised rigorous austerities for 12 years before he attained enlightenment.

Awakening

Historical period of renewed interest in religion

The term "awakening" has also been used in a Christian context, namely during the Great Awakenings, several periods of religious revival in American religious history. Historians and theologians identified three or four periods of increased religious enthusiasm occurring between the early eighteenth century and the late nineteenth century. Each of these "Great Awakenings" was characterised by widespread revivals led by evangelical Ministers and a sharp increase of interest in religion.

Illumination

Another equivalent term for awakening is Illumination. Illuminationism is a doctrine according to which the process of human thought needs to be aided by divine grace.

Augustine was an important proponent of Illuminationism, stating that everything we know is taught to us by God as He casts His light over the world saying that "The mind needs to be enlightened by light from outside itself, so that it can participate in truth. 'You will light my lamp, Lord' and 'You hear nothing true from me which you have not first told me.'"

Experience

A common reference in many western cultures is the notion of "enlightenment *experience*". It was popularised by the Transcendentalists, and exported to Asia via missionaries.

It is fundamentally a variety of diverse concepts found in Hindu texts like the Vedas, the Upanishads and the Bhagavad Gita. Nevertheless, the notion of religious experience has gained widespread use in the study of religion, and is extensively researched. The word "enlightenment" is not generally used in Christian contexts for religious understanding or insight. More commonly used term in the Christian tradition is 'revelation'.

Spirituality and Enlightenment- The Knowledge Management Connection

Some conclusions the author would like to draw from the information shared in the foregoing passages on spirituality are as follows:

1. A vast amount of literature is available on spiritual concepts like awakening, enlightenment, *mukhthi* or freedom, soul consciousness, illumination and so on.
2. The knowledge is available in explicit form in texts, scriptures and documents in several religions and across cultures spanning several communities around the world.
3. All religions talk about enlightenment and awakening as the prime tools for God Realisation and eventually the purpose of life.
4. The transformation which comes about in human beings while aspiring to reach out to the unknown God or Shakti is through a process of enlightenment experience of the self and surrender to the Brahman, the cosmic energy source controlling creation.
5. Methodologies and practices such as yoga in Hinduism, meditation and prayer in almost all religions are tools which enable attainment of the ultimate experience of bliss and God Realisation liberating us from the bondage of birth, death and sufferings due to sensual attachments.

The reader has been provided just enough knowledge in the foregoing paragraphs, so that he can read, acquire more, use, re-use, experience, share, gain more knowledge and wisdom to discover the truth about life. That is the purpose with which the author has written this chapter and in turn, this book. The author wishes to conclude by saying, 'Enjoy reading this book, Acquire and Manage Knowledge, so that you become wiser, happier and more peaceful to live life more purposefully.'

GOD BLESS YOU

References

1. Wikipedia, The Free Encyclopedia, 2014.
2. *'Does God exist? Here are six straightforward reasons to believe that God is really there.'* By Marilyn Adamson.
3. R. E. D. Clark, *Creation* (London: Tyndale Press, 1946), p. 20. The Wonders of God's Creation, Moody Institute of Science (Chicago, IL).
4. Hugh Davson, *Physiology of the Eye,* 5th ed (New York: McGraw Hill, 1991).
5. Robert Jastrow; "Message from Professor Robert Jastrow"; *LeaderU.com;* 2002.
6. Steven Weinberg; *The First Three Minutes: A Modern View of the Origin of the Universe;* (Basic Books, 1998).
7. Dinesh D'Souza, *What's So Great about Christianity;* (Regnery Publishing, Inc, 2007, chapter 11).
8. Richard Feynman, *The Meaning of It All: Thoughts of a Citizen-Scientist* (New York: Basic Books, 1998), 43.

Bibliography

1. Malhotra, Yogesh. (1998). Knowledge Management, Knowledge Organisations and Knowledge Workers: A View from the Front Lines [WWW document]. URL: http://www. brint. com/interview/maeil. htm
2. Dr Viswanathan Gopalan, 'Knowledge Management, Challenges in the IT Era', ISSN Journal, 2014, ASM Group, Pune.
3. Rebecca O. Barclay, Philip C. Murray, What is knowledge management, http://www. media-access. com/whatis. html
4. David Gurteen, Creating a knowledge sharing culture, February 1999, http://www. gurteen. com
5. Thomas H. Davenport, Knowledge management at Ernst & Young, 1997.
6. Tiwana Amrit, the knowledge management toolkit 2th, Prentice Hall PTR 2002.
7. Wikipedia, The Free Encyclopedia, 2014.
8. David J. Skyrme, The 3Cs of knowledge Sharing:Culture, Co-operation and Commitment, August 2002 http://www. skyrme. com/updates/u64_fl. htm
9. Dr Viswanathan Gopalan, 'Motivation-The Essence of Living', Gyan Books Pvt Ltd, New Delhi, 2014.
10. Dr Anjali Ghanekar, "Organisational behaviour, Concepts and Cases", Everest Publishing House, Pune, Eighth Edition, 2002.

11. Dr Viswanathan Gopalan, 'Stress Management and the Science of Living', VIPSAR, Indore, ISSN Journal, 2013 June.
12. Stress Management - Helpguide. org
13. *www. helpguide. org/mental/stress_management_relief_coping. htm*
14. A.H. Maslow, "Motivation and Personality", Harper and Bros, New York, 1954.
15. D. C. McClellend, "The Achieving", D. Nostrandco. Inc, Princeton, N. J., 1961.
16. Frederick Hertzberg, Bernard Mausner and Barbara Shydermann, "The Motivation to Work", 2nd Edition, John Wiley and Son. Inc, New York, 1959.
17. Keith Davis and J. W. Newstrom, "Human Behaviour at Work-Organisational Behaviour", Mcgraw-Hill, New York, 1989.
18. Fred Luthens, "Organisational Behaviour", Mcgraw-Hill Inc., New York, 1995.
19. Dr Anjali Ghanekar, "Organisational behaviour, Concepts and Cases", Everest Publishing House, Pune, Eighth Edition, 2002.
20. David C. McClellend, "Managing Motivation to Expand Human Freedom", American Psychologist, 1978.
21. Fred Luthens and Robert Krietner, 'The Management of Behavioural Contingencies", Personnel, July 1974.
22. Frederick Hertzberg, "One More Time, How do you Motivate Employees", Harvard Business Review, Selected Articles, Reprint, Motivation, 1970.
23. Dr Viswanathan Gopalan, 'Motivation-The Essence of Living' Gyan Books Pvt Ltd, New Delhi, 2014.
24. Dr Viswanathan Gopalan, "Motivation and Its Relevance to Productivity". Thesis for Ph. D, Pune University, 2001.
25. Dr Viswanathan Gopalan, "Motivating Knowledeg Worker". ISSN-Journal Symbiosis, 2012.

26. Dr Viswanathan Gopalan, "The Significance of Motivation with regard to Productivity", ISSN Journal, Amity University, Lucknow, 2014.
27. http://www. psychologies. co. uk/love/can-you-learn-to-love-anyone.
28. http://www. eharmony. com/dating-advice/dating/common-love-myths-and-how-they-affect-your-dating-life/#. Ul65gJlDv2lhttp://www. marcandangel. com/2012/06/13/ 15-relationship-truths-for-tough-times/http://www. eharmony. com/dating-advice/relationships/eight-valuable-love-lessons-you-need-to-know/#. Ul65fZlDv2l
29. *'Does God exist? Here are six straightforward reasons to believe that God is really there.'* By Marilyn Adamson.
30. R.E.D. Clark, *Creation* (London: Tyndale Press, 1946), p. 20. The Wonders of God's Creation, Moody Institute of Science (Chicago, IL).
31. Hugh Davson, *Physiology of the Eye,* 5th ed (New York: McGraw Hill, 1991).
32. Robert Jastrow; "Message from Professor Robert Jastrow"; *LeaderU. com;* 2002.
33. Steven Weinberg; *The First Three Minutes: A Modern View of the Origin of the Universe;* (Basic Books, 1998).
34. Dinesh D'Souza, *What's So Great about Christianity;* (Regnery Publishing, Inc, 2007, chapter 11).
35. Richard Feynman, *The Meaning of It All: Thoughts of a Citizen-Scientist* (New York: Basic Books, 1998), 43.

Index